"The first time I heard Chris Zane speak about customer service and creating lifetime customers, it changed my thinking forever. Get ready for a similar experience as you read this book."

—**STEVE CHURCH,** Senior Vice President, Chief Business Development and Process Officer, Avnet, Inc.

"Chris Zane's bold—and practical—approach to cultivating lifetime customers holds valuable lessons for businesses large and small. Through a series of engaging stories, Chris shares his recipe for experiences that offer more than what customers expect. And he shows us how to build deep emotional bonds, even in the face of material price premiums. A fascinating read and an excellent testament to the power of customer centricity and unconditional service guarantees!"

—**JULIE MOLL,** SVP, Global Brand Strategy and Research, Marriott International

"Blend an unrivaled entrepreneurial spirit, a passion for delivering quality service, a highly creative mind, and a big dose of 'street smarts,' and what you get is Chris Zane. *Reinventing the Wheel* is a marvelous book that will teach you and inspire you."

—**DR. LEONARD L. BERRY,** Distinguished Professor of Marketing, Texas A&M, and Author of *Management Lessons from Mayo Clinic*

"Zane's relentless pursuit of building life-long customers by reinventing the wheel is truly inspiring. Watch out bike dealers of America—Zane's may be coming to your town next!"

—**ROBERT ZOLLARS,** Chairman & CEO, Vocera Communications, Inc.

"*Reinventing the Wheel* is an inspirational story of how to look beyond the horizon of instant rewards in order to plant the seeds of deep brand loyalty and customer lifetime relationships.

— KIM GRAVELL, VP, Innovation & Strategy Management, Cardinal Health Supply Solutions

"*Reinventing the Wheel* tells a story of linking extraordinary service to value for the customers, the Zane's employees, the communities it touches, and ultimately the culture and success of his business. It is hard to read the account of Zane's service journey without stimulating ideas for my business and my life."

— CHRIS MELOCIK, Senior Vice President, Integration & Process Improvement, Republic Services, Inc.

"Chris Zane, a hands-on entrepreneur, brings novel next practices to life and also demonstrates how to execute practices that others have only talked or written about. More than a case study, this book is a must-read for entrepreneurs, managers, marketers, and others wanting to grow their business through non conventional and truly innovative investments in customers."

— STEPHEN BROWN, PhD, Professor and Executive Director, Center for Services Leadership, W. P. Carey School of Business, Arizona State University

"*Reinventing the Wheel* is the employee guidebook behind the outstanding success of Zane's Cycles. Chris Zane has shared his strategies to create customer experiences that establish lifelong customers and change the game for his competition. This book is full of examples that are relevant for both small and large companies focused on growth, customer loyalty and competitive differentiation."

— STEVE CLARK, vice president, Siemens Industry Solutions

"What is an archetype?

Chris Zane's *Reinventing the Wheel* provides a step by step business success roadmap for readers that will educate both the neophyte and the seasoned entrepreneur. His objective in this book is to share with the reader his secrets behind the 'Science of Creating Lifetime Customers.'

The title and age-old phrase—*Reinventing the Wheel*—might seem like a cliché to some, but in my estimation Chris's book is bound to become an archetype and ideal example of the 'how to do it' for long-term customer-r elationship building in any business.

In writing this book, Chris taps his years of experience from his first bike shop in his teenage years up until today, where he has built a nationally recognized retail operation and distribution system used by some of America's largest corporate organizations. He transitions from teaching you how to 'define your business' to 'determining your strategy for a winning proposition' to 'focusing on continuing improvement once your business model is working.'

I have known of Chris and his achievements for years, yet this book was a joy for me to read and to learn from, advancing through each page on the Amazon Kindle with an anticipation and an appetite for more.

His combination of simple talk and sensible explanation, combined with true-life stories, makes his first book a simple read. I will keep Chris's *Reinventing the Wheel* on my desktop for my personal reference and to lend out to our company's future brand builders."

—**JIM ISSLER,** President and CEO of H.H. Brown
(a Berkshire Hathaway company)

CHRIS ZANE

reinventing
the
wheel

• the science of creating •
lifetime customers

BenBella Books, Inc.
Dallas, Texas

Copyright © 2011 by Chris Zane

BenBella Books, Inc.

10300 N. Central Expressway, Suite 400

Dallas, TX 75231

www.benbellabooks.com

Send feedback to feedback@benbellabooks.com

Printed in the United States of America

10 9 8 7 6 5 4 3 2 1

Library of Congress Cataloging-in-Publication Data is available for this title.

978-1-935618-15-7

Editorial contributions by Darren Dahl

Copyediting by Deb Kirkby

Proofreading by Michael Fedison and Sara Cassidy

Index by Tracy Wilson-Burns

Cover design by Michael Fusco

Text design and composition by Pauline Neuwirth, Neuwirth & Associates, Inc.

Printed by Bang Printing

Distributed by Perseus Distribution

(www.perseusdistribution.com)

To place orders through Perseus Distribution:

Tel: 800-343-4499

Fax: 800-351-5073

E-mail: orderentry@perseusbooks.com

Significant discounts for bulk sales are available. Please contact Glenn Yeffeth at glenn@benbellabooks.com or (214) 750-3628.

With love to my wife, Kathleen,
who endlessly encourages and supports my passion;
to my sons, Ian, Charlie, and Oliver;
and my parents, John and Patricia, for their inspiration and
willingness to agree to such an unbelievable request

contents

introduction

xi

· 1 ·

what business are you in?

1

· 2 ·

building lifetime relationships

25

· 3 ·

a winning proposition

55

· 4 ·

planting seeds

79

· 5 ·

stretch your comfort zone

93

· 6 ·

game-changing tactics

115

· 7 ·

focus on continuous improvement

137

· 8 ·

hiring help

159

· 9 ·

mix it up

179

· 10 ·

think nationally, act locally

193

index

201

about the author

205

introduction

How much is one customer worth to your business? For me, it's $12,500. That means that my average customer will spend $12,500 on my products and services over his or her lifetime, $5,000 of which is profit. Of course, the only chance I have of ever seeing that kind of return on the relationship is if that customer keeps coming back and back again. Better yet, I want customers to come back with their kids, their relatives, and five friends. To put it another way, I need to develop a trusting relationship with customers right from the get-go—one that I hope will last a lifetime—so that they can see how passionate we are about what we do.

Although I may own Zane's Cycles, a bike shop similar to the one down the street from you, I consider myself to be in the experience business, not the selling stuff business. And what do I mean by that? Think about a seven-year-old kid's first bike. With the power to pedal around the neighborhood all on his or her own, that two-wheeler, whether it has training wheels or not, probably represents the first real freedom that kid has ever experienced away from the parental grip. Or consider the guy who lives next door to you who wants to lose some weight. His bike is more than two wheels and a frame—it really represents a weight-loss and feel-good-about-himself program. Consider the retiree who uses her bike to explore all those national parks she never made time for while she was working. For her, that bike is like a passport to adventure. No matter how you look at it, we aren't simply selling bikes but something much, much more exciting. But make no mistake—anyone can sell that kid or that newly retired woman a bike. That's why we go about the whole process in reverse.

At Zane's, we've failed if all we've done is complete a transaction with a customer. For us to be successful, we need to show our customers that we are *Reinventing the Wheel*. And that reinvention starts as soon as one of our customers walks into one of our stores or receives one of our bikes as part of a corporate rewards program. That's how we have grown a neighborhood bike shop in Branford, Connecticut, into the foundation of a national bike store chain with multiple corporate customers and annual revenues in excess of $15 million. And we're not done yet: our annual sales continue to grow briskly at the rate of 23.5 percent a year. Although it's easy for me to describe how we think about our relationships with customers and partners today, and what keeps them coming back and back again, it's not like I had everything figured out from the start. It actually took a brief bout of failure before I truly came to understand the challenge of reinventing the wheel.

· a painful lesson ·

It all started innocently enough back in 1985. At the time, I was the twenty-year-old owner of a classic Main Street retail bike shop in Branford, Connecticut. I bought the shop at the age of sixteen from the previous owner with the help of my parents and my grandfather, who actually loaned me $23,000 from his money-market savings account. (Unwilling to diminish his income, he charged me the same 15 percent interest on the loan as he was earning from his savings account.) Four years later, the business was growing like gangbusters, pulling in about $100,000 in revenue at that point. But, like most twenty year olds, I was itching to find my place in the world. I had always loved working on bikes, but running a single shop didn't seem bold enough. I was hungry for a new challenge— I wanted to do something *really* big. That's when I started thinking that my customers really wanted to buy more than just bikes; they wanted someone, namely me, to supply all their outdoor gear. A few months later, after swapping most of the equity I had earned from the bike shop over its first few years for inventory like tents and sleeping bags and a down payment on a lease for a new location in a downtown New Haven mall, Zane's Outdoor was born. And by the end of the store's second week, I knew we were sunk.

A big part of the problem was that the location I had chosen had virtually zero foot traffic; customers didn't even know we were there. That meant I had all this great stuff sitting around on the shelves, eating up space, losing value by the day. Still worse, because we weren't turning anything over, we simply couldn't generate any cash flow. And so, after the holidays, just ten weeks after we started, I pulled the plug. The mall had given me an option to renew my lease and I opted out for the simple reason that in less than three months, we had lost $100,000. That meant that the Outdoor store had not only eaten up all the profits from the cycle shop, but I couldn't even pay my vendors back for the merchandise they had provided to me on credit. So, I shipped back all the gear I could—my vendors were happy just to get something back from me—and hauled the rest back to my original cycle shop. I sat in the back room with my chin in my hand, surrounded by stacks of boxes of unsold tents and knapsacks, which served as a looming reminder of my failure. My brown hair had become mottled with gray and, for one of the few times in my life, I felt depressed.

For the next two years, as things continued to spiral downward, I decided it was time to change things up. I came to the conclusion that April 1987 was going to be the end. I didn't tell anyone, but I had made plans to head back to college. All that was left to do was hold a giant blowout sale, liquidate our entire inventory, and use the proceeds to pay back the $25,000 I still owed my vendors. With a plan in place, I felt better and the newfound energy I found within helped me spring into action. I rented a bunch of outdoor tents and stocked them with all our old stuff. Then I called up all the local newspapers and placed ads to promote the upcoming event, calling it our Big Wheel Sale. It would be a fitting last hurrah.

Only that's not how it turned out. To my utter surprise, the sale was a huge success—thousands of people from all over the state showed up and snapped up everything we put out there. We ended up clearing $45,000 in a single weekend. Although I was mostly baffled by the turn of events, I got to thinking again. Even after I squared everything up with my vendors, I would still have $20,000 in my pocket. Maybe we could try again, I thought, only this time I would let my customers lead me instead of trying to guess what they wanted. As a matter of fact, I needed to do even more: I needed to make them the focal point of the entire operation. With my new plan in place, I felt rejuvenated. I plowed what I had left into new inventory and refocused on serving our customers and not just selling them stuff. By July, just three months after our restart, our annual sales were up to $325,000. We were on our way—and it's been a terrific journey ever since. Today, more than twenty years later, we're a $15 million business and on the cusp of even greater things.

You could say that the Big Wheel Sale was a turning point for both the business and for me as a businessman. We still hold that sale every April, generating more than 15 percent of our annual retail revenue on that single spring weekend. That sale is a huge draw for our business, and we spend half our advertising budget on promoting it as the kickoff to the cycling season. Not only do folks from all over New England show up, but we also have former employees—those kids that used to work for me in high school who are now doctors, lawyers, and engineers—flocking back to take part in the hoopla by helping out for the weekend. It has become our *de facto* alumni weekend. But more important, it's our chance to connect with new customers—our chance to lay the foundation for what we hope will be hundreds, even thousands, of new lifetime relationships. The sale is our opportunity to introduce new customers—and remind our current ones—to our programs like lifetime free service, upgrades, and whatever other new and exciting service offerings we have recently rolled out. Our goal, which has become our mantra of sorts, is to sell our customers an unexpected experience they will never forget.

The success of that first Big Wheel Sale also helped me shift from thinking that my business was a job to understanding that it was a game—a game where you could change the rules on your competitors. Thinking that way is how Zane's expanded from a retail bike shop into a player in the world of corporate rewards programs, where we now supply the bikes that companies like American Express and Marriott give away to their most valuable customers. This division has grown to become a huge component of our business, and it's something that few, if any, of our competitors have been able to copy because we changed the rules.

We aren't better than our competitors because we offer better stuff—everybody has access to cool toys like carbon-fiber frames or aerodynamic wheels. We're better than our competitors because we differentiate ourselves by offering more service than most customers consider reasonable. In other words, our goal is simply to blow them away with our attention to detail as soon as we meet them. The job of every Zane's employee is not just to sell stuff; it is to build relationships with our customers by servicing them in a manner they have rarely experienced before.

 The job of every Zane's employee is not just to sell stuff; it is to build relationships with our customers by servicing them in a manner they have rarely experienced before.

I keep preaching this lesson to myself and to my employees because this is what creates loyalty to the Zane's brand and lifetime customers. And that's not to say we've got it all figured out. I want my employees to keep pushing the envelope, keep experimenting with how we can make our customer relationships even better. After all, every potential customer is worth that same $12,500 to our business.

• it's not rocket science •

As we embark on our newest challenge—rolling out Zane's Cycles nationally—this mantra of building lifetime customer relationships is something we'll be hammering home over and over again. And it's why I keep thinking back to the lessons I learned through the experience of running Zane's Outdoor for those ten weeks once upon a time.

In that light, I actually have two goals in writing this book. Up until this point, when Zane's was simply a one-location business, I could serve as both mentor and guide to new and veteran employees alike. Now that we're planning on opening more than a hundred locations over the next decade, I simply can't serve that same role. Rather than going through the painful-sounding process of cloning myself, I hope that this book will become an employee handbook of sorts, a guide all Zane's employees can refer back to to remind themselves what makes our business tick.

My other goal in writing this book is to show you, the reader, that no matter what kind of business you run, you should be in the relationship-building and experience-selling business because that is how you will find the greatest success. And rather than learn from a textbook, you'll be able to use Zane's as a practical case study in what to do and not to do. Fortunately, a bike shop is a great example because just about every person on the planet has had an experience in one.

This isn't something I knew from the start—it took the sting of the Zane's Outdoor experience, along with many other successes and failures, to learn this lesson for myself. By providing insight into the process of *Reinventing the Wheel*, I'm offering you a chance to put your own learning curve into fast forward, to learn from our experiences what it means to win the trust of a lifetime customer. Join me as I show you how we do it.

· 1 ·

what business
are you in?

LIKE EVERYONE, I occasionally suffer a bad day at work. I don't know, maybe I didn't sleep well or I spilled my coffee in my lap or whatever. Whenever one of those days comes around, though, I have a foolproof way to change things up. I dig up a print-out of an e-mail I received a few years back from Patrick, a very dissatisfied customer.

Titling his note "Frustrated with Zane's," Patrick wrote me a short novel detailing a series of bad experiences that he had suffered when buying a new Trek bicycle from us. In his well-written note, Patrick explained how much he had been looking forward to purchasing his new bike. He was returning to riding after taking a fifteen-year break and he was looking for a bike that he could use for both commuting and some off-road riding. He had heard good things about our store and decided to buy his new bike from us. Patrick then explained to me that he had made three visits to the store over the period of just a few months—and the experience related to each visit was worse than the one before it.

Our first offense was offering very little help when Patrick was trying to find the bike that best fit his riding style and body type. The second offense was when a Zane's employee apparently tried to charge him $220 more than he owed when he returned to the shop to pick up his new Trek 4300 Disc. The third affront was when Patrick dropped off his Trek a few weeks later for a tune-up, expecting that the job would be done within the hour as a sales clerk had told him over the phone. After browsing about the store for a while, he checked in to ask about the progress on the job only to learn that the job actually wouldn't be done for several days. To make matters even worse, if you can believe it, at this point Patrick learned that, because no one had helped him in choosing his bike on his initial visit, he had bought too large a frame—a 19.5-inch instead of an 18-inch—and it was then well past the thirty-day return guarantee we give our customers, so he was stuck with it.

As a summary to his note, Patrick went to great lengths to tell me that not only had he found each of his interactions with Zane's associates to be underwhelming, but he dug the knife in deeper by telling me that he had decided to buy his next bike from one of my arch competitors, a shop that treated him far better than Zane's did. Patrick, we can all agree, obviously did not have a compelling customer experience at Zane's.

Now, as anyone who works with customers knows, there's nothing worse than when customers are unhappy. But what do you do about it? In most cases, you could either try to make that customer into a happier camper or you could simply chalk him or her off as just a casualty of doing business. But at Zane's, that's not good enough. The happiness of our customers is the lifeblood of our business. There was never any question that we needed to make things right for Patrick. To get things started, I forwarded Patrick's e-mail on to Tom Girard, my store manager, along with a note of my own that said, "This is all yours." I knew Tom would do what was needed to change Patrick's perception of what it meant to purchase a bike from Zane's.

Sure enough, a few days later, I received another e-mail from Patrick, this one titled, "Completely Won Over by Zane's." This time, you can practically see Patrick's smile as he wrote about how Tom had invited him back to the store to refit him for a new bike—at no charge. He then mentioned how comfortable Tom and Greg, another Zane's employee, had made him feel when asking questions about the kind of bike he should get so he could feel confident in making his decision. Patrick also admitted to being blown away when Tom threw in a few extras like toe clips and a handlebar light at no charge. He went on to write:

"As I drove away with my new bike and accessories, I realized that this was the single best customer experience I've ever had . . . I came into Zane's having not ridden a mountain bike in fifteen years. Now I'm twenty-seven, but out on the trails I still feel like I'm twelve. Thank you so much for your kindness and generosity in the past few days. I am now proud to call myself a loyal Zane's customer. I look forward to telling all my friends about my incredible service experience and encouraging them to patronize your store. I, for one, look forward to shopping at Zane's for years to come.

We delivered an experience that the customer described as the single best customer service experience of his life ... But our goal at Zane's is not just to deliver that kind of experience to the occasional unhappy customers; we want every one of our customers to leave our store with that exact same feeling, whether they bought a $5,000 bike that Lance Armstrong rides, picked up a $20 hand pump, or simply stopped in to say hello."

The key point that I make to Zane's employees when I show them Patrick's e-mails or tell them this story is that we were not only able to salvage a relationship with an unhappy customer, but, more important, we delivered an experience that the customer described as the single best customer service experience of his life. But our goal at Zane's is not just to deliver that kind of experience to the occasional unhappy customers; we want every one of our customers to leave our store with that exact same feeling, whether they bought a $5,000 bike that Lance Armstrong rides, picked up a $20 hand pump, or simply stopped in to say hello. Our competitive advantage, that continuous focus on reinventing the wheel, is not in the things that we sell—it's everything embodied in those two e-mails from a formerly dissatisfied customer.

• great customer service •
trumps cheap prices

When I started Zane's Cycles more than twenty-five years ago, I was surrounded by at least seventeen different competitors in my county—everyone from big-box retailers like Toys "R" Us to other bike shops like mine on Main Street. And every one of them had an advantage over me. Here I was, sixteen years old, working after high school to build and repair bikes. I was the mechanic, head of marketing, and the guy who cleaned the bathroom, all rolled into one. It didn't take much for my competitors to beat me on everything, from the size of their showrooms and the variety of their displays to their wide inventory selection and even the prices of their bikes.

The big retailers at the time—Bradlees, Caldor, Grants, and Child World—had sophisticated internal systems in place that made them as efficient as possible, which allowed them to sell their products as cheaply as possible. Competing on price, even in the pre-Walmart era, would clearly not work well, especially because I was paying more for my products in the first place. When I first started the business, prior to securing a direct relationship with bicycle manufacturers, I was buying unassembled Columbia bikes from big-box retailers, assembling them, then trying to turn them around and sell them for more than I paid. Today, by leveraging newer and cheaper technology, Walmart makes competing on price nearly impossible.

Clearly, I had to find some other way to differentiate myself. I credit my mom, who often manned the shop's counter for me when I was at school, for telling me, "Chris, if you deliver great customer service, you'll stay in business. If you don't, you won't." That piece of simple advice helped me understand that I could set the company apart from my competitors by focusing on giving customers superior service and building long-term relationships with them. If I stopped thinking I was in the "selling stuff" business and instead that I was in the "selling experiences" business, I could attract those customers who weren't 100 percent price driven. If I gave them more than they expected with a positive experience attached to it, they would see value in paying $179 to buy a bike from Zane's as opposed to plunking down $99 for the same bike at Child World.

Of course, I was scared to death of going out of business—which is always a great motivator to try new things. I was small potatoes, but that didn't mean I had to stay that way. But I soon realized that what I was trying to do wasn't all that difficult. Rather than obsessing over textbook concepts like inventory turns or the cost of goods sold, all I had to do was think about how to make our customers think good things about us. That customer sentiment would be the determining factor in whether we would ultimately become successful or not.

Now, twenty-five years later, I can stand back and see what a tremendous return on investment that decision was. That's why we still benchmark our success not on the products we offer or the price we sell them at but on how well we connect with our customers through the services we provide them. And the only way we can stay focused on doing that is by emphasizing to our staff again and again that we're not in the business of selling *stuff* but in the business of selling *experiences.*

• what business are you in? •

Every entrepreneur or business owner has this same opportunity to offer extraordinary customer service. But before you can, you need to ask yourself a critical question: what business are you in?

Consider a story a friend told me about the power tool manufacturer Black & Decker. A few years ago, the company hired a consultant to help them strategize ways to grow their power drill business. That consultant spent months surveying carpenters and contractors all over the country about what they look for when buying a drill. He asked them questions like: Do they prefer more torque or less? Would they rather rely on power cords or batteries? The list went on and on, detailing every gadget option the company could possibly dream up. When the consultant finally tabulated all the replies and presented his findings to management, the results surprised just about everyone: contractors don't buy a drill because of its gadgets but because they need a hole in a piece of wood. In other words, Black & Decker wasn't in the drill-selling business; they were in the hole-making business.

Kodak, the film company, has a similar story. A few years back, they were losing market share to their rival, Fuji. So Kodak, too, hired a consultant to see what kinds of high-tech film they should be investing in to boost their sales. The answer, the consultant told Kodak management, was to stop selling film and start selling the experience of capturing the moment. And so the Kodak Moment was born.

But the company hasn't stopped there. As the business has shifted from film to digital photography, Kodak has shifted with it. Kodak now makes products like cameras that you pop into a cradle so that all you have to do is push a button to print out the latest snapshots from your vacation, kid's birthday, or whatever.

If you buy a competitor's product, on the other hand, you might have to learn how to connect the camera to your computer with a cable and open the right software before you even get the chance to print—if you can even find where the pictures got downloaded onto your hard drive. With the Kodak approach, the typical grandmother can actually print out the pictures of her grandkids without the need to figure out a computer. That means Kodak is really selling ease of use and a sense of confidence to people who might otherwise be intimidated by all this talk about digital pictures. Focus on the customer experience rather than on the product.

In a similar vein, we at Zane's sell the equivalent of holes, moments, and feelings of self-confidence instead of bikes. As soon as our mind-set shifts to thinking about selling spokes, rubber, and carbon fiber, we, too, will lose our edge. This same principle applies to every other business out there; if you can shift your thinking away from just selling a product or a service and into establishing intimate relationships with your customers, you'll find an easy way to drive your competitors nuts. As another example, I can point to Mitchells, a high-end men's clothing store down I-95 in Westport, Connecticut, where I spend a considerable amount of money. Jack Mitchell, who now runs the business his dad started in 1958, actually wrote an excellent book called *Hug Your Customers* (and a follow-up called *Hug Your People*), and when he says that, he really means it. Well, sort of.

Hugging his customers, Jack says, has nothing to do with being touchy-feely around them and everything to do with offering them over-the-top service. For Jack, that means serving coffee and bagels in the store and giving away hot dogs in the parking lot on summer Saturdays. It also means going to customers' homes to help tie their bow ties for gala events or even offering a customer the coat off his back if that's the only one left in the store in his size, preferred style, and color. I also keep buying my suits from Jack (actually from Joe Derosa, the sales specialist who takes care of me) because I know that when I rip one, which I will inevitably do, they will be right there to make the repair. And when I pick it up, it's pressed and ready to go. Sure, I could purchase less expensive, lower quality suits if I went elsewhere. But the positive experience I get from buying from Jack and his team allows me to justify paying whatever they need to charge; plus this ensures they'll be around to serve my needs in the future.

This notion of selling an experience doesn't just apply to retail businesses. Consider the story of a couple of guys I met after a speaking engagement I gave at a national convention a few years back. The two men, who run a snow-plowing business, wondered if they, too, could really offer their customers something extraordinary. "What could we do to surprise our customers?" one of the guys asked me. "Our business doesn't work the same way yours does."

"You are in the same business I am and I'll prove it," I replied. "Do you ever bring in your customers' trash cans after you finish plowing?" I asked them.

"All the time," he said.

"Well, how about the next time you do it, you slap a removable sticker on the cans that has your company logo on it, promoting the thoughtful nature of your company?" I suggested. "That way, your customer will know you brought the cans in and see value in making their life easier."

He loved it. How many other snowplow guys think to remind their customers about these little extras? The point is that by doing more, by creating a positive and unexpected experience, along with a gentle reminder of what you did, you're changing the relationship you have with your customer. Think that customer will call anyone else ever again? To put it another way, when you give your customers more than they expect, do more than just sell them a product or service, and tell them about it, they'll never leave you.

• making the connection •

The first part of selling an experience, then, is finding a way to connect with your customer—to find that thing that will absolutely blow them away. The problem is that most people don't even know how to get started. For instance, one of my pet peeves is when the clerk or salesperson asks me, "Can I help you?" whenever I walk into a store. "Of course you can," I usually mutter to myself whenever I hear this, "why else do you think I'm in here?" The only thing more annoying is when you walk up to someone stocking shelves at a grocery or hardware store and ask them for help, only to receive a look that says, "Why are you bothering me? Can't you see that I'm busy?" Hey, man, I'm asking for help so that I can buy something so that you can have a job—you should be happy that I'm here.

I'm amazed that businesses don't spend more time with their employees stressing how important it is to make those customers feel valued. Any organization that fails to coach its employees not to say things like "Can I help you?" also fails to recognize that it has encouraged its employees to turn on autopilot, so they are just responding in the way a robot would.

At the same time, all the money businesses waste on building the appearance that they care about their customers also blows me away. For example, Southwest Airlines sends out birthday cards to its customers or at least to those customers whose addresses the company has collected. People tend to have different reactions to opening a card that just says "Happy Birthday! From your friends at Southwest Airlines." That's it: nothing more, nothing less. For me, I'm wondering where the discount flight coupon is—or even a free drink. Otherwise, why would they waste the forty-four-cent stamp to send me this? My wife, on the other hand, might appreciate that this airline remembered her birthday. I'm sure she would have been more appreciative if I had actually remembered to get her a card myself. Maybe I'm upset because Southwest made me look bad!

On a more serious note, the Southwest example actually demonstrates an important phenomenon when it comes to finding a variety of ways to connect with your customers. Martin Mende, a friend of mine who recently earned his PhD at the W.P. Carey School of Business at Arizona State University, has gathered mountains of research on consumer behavior and has come to the conclusion that, when it comes to judging reactions to marketing campaigns like the one Southwest uses, the majority of customers can actually be broken down into four categories. One of these categories, apparently the one to which I belong, is filled with customers who won't be at all responsive to personalized mass mailings such as these. My wife, on the other hand, belongs to the second category of people who appreciate them. Customers that make up the other two categories aren't at all sure what to make of these kinds of mailings. Maybe some of them like the idea of a company making the effort to reach out to them, but the companies also need something more substantial than a postcard to do it.

When Martin told me the results of his research, I was fascinated: of course, not every customer is the same, but once a customer is categorized into a "personality box," future surveys reinforce that their preferences rarely change. If we at Zane's really wanted to connect with each and every one of our customers, we would need to employ a variety of methods to accomplish that goal. That's why we now spend so much of our time finding ways to make stronger connections with customers based on their personal preferences for building relationships.

With that goal in mind, I have traveled the world both for business and pleasure and I've concluded that no matter where you find yourself in the world, people everywhere all seem to fit neatly into Martin's categories. A world of opportunity awaits both researchers and practitioners like me if we can use Martin's work to find the best ways to approach and connect with customers the world over. That means that if we can find ways to reach out to customers in a store in Lucerne, Switzerland, we can do the same in Branford, Connecticut, or in New York City.

As soon as a customer walks in the door of one of our shops anywhere in the country or anywhere in the world, I want a Zane's employee to start looking for clues on how he or she can approach that customer in a conversational manner to make him or her feel immediately comfortable and relaxed. One way could be using the weather outside to make a connection—suggesting, for example that all that rain out there will sure make for some fun riding tomorrow out in the mud.

As a first step in that direction, I invested $3,000 a few years back to install a fourteen-foot-long mahogany coffee bar in the bike shop, where we serve free coffee and bottles of Snapple. If you're a customer sitting at the bar, you can look through a plate-glass window and watch our repair team at work while you enjoy a refreshing beverage. Does it get more relaxing than that? Not only does the bar give our regular customers a place to come, hang out, and talk about cycling, it creates energy inside the shop that new customers walking through the door can tap into.

If you think about it, businesses are either living or dying entities. You know how uncomfortable it can be to walk into a retail environment where you're the only customer and where every eye is focused on you alone. Creepy. Whenever I feel that, my first instinct is to walk back out the door. But who could feel creepy when the nutty smell of gourmet

coffee literally pulls you in? For the little it costs me to supply the coffee and the drinks—about five dollars a day—the
coffee bar is invaluable in the way it alleviates any anxieties
our customers might have when they walk into our store.

But the worst thing a Zane's employee can do (other
than saying "Can I help you?") is to pass judgment on what
a customer might need that day. There is nothing worse
than a salesperson trying to show off to the customer or
prove how much he or she knows about our available bikes.
You know the drill: you stand there and listen to someone
run his or her mouth about how great this bike is or how all
their friends swear by this other one. Who knew buying a
bike could be like visiting a used car lot, right?

It's a waste of time. That customer already assumes we
know what we're talking about—that's why he or she has
stopped in at our store in the first place. But that doesn't
mean that we want to pull a hard sell on customers, telling
them that they absolutely have to have that very expensive,
full-suspension mountain bike, if they never actually intend
to do the kind of off-road riding for which that kind of bike
is built. One of the mandates for anyone working the floor
at a Zane's shop is never tell a customer something about a
bike or a part without also telling them a story about why it
matters to him or her personally.

For example, a salesperson can't just tell our casual rider
customers that they absolutely need tires that can be inflated
to 90 psi. I can picture that customer's face, just nodding
along, too intimidated to ask what in the heck 90 psi means
(pounds per square inch). Instead, we need to explain to

our customer why 90 psi matters—because it makes the tires super hard, which means they'll roll faster than softer tires and lead to fewer flat tires as well. But even relating those kinds of details hardly matter if we haven't already established a relationship with that customer.

For Zane's to be successful as a business, we need to connect with the emotional aspects of buying a bike. When parents come into the shop, for example, we want to help them imagine what it's like to be seven years old again, taking that first spin on a bike without training wheels. Your dad or mom is holding on to you and then—wham!—you're off on your own. What a feeling of freedom to be pedaling beyond the grasp of your parents, to be far enough away that, for the first time in your young life, you're making your own decisions (which one hopes don't involve crashing head over handlebars into the pavement). When you can create a conversation with a customer that starts to sound something like this, the worst thing a salesperson can do is to begin yakking about the quality of the bike's brake lever or something; those details are completely irrelevant. All that dad or mom wants to focus on is how much fun their child is going to have over the next bunch of months riding his or her new bike every free minute possible.

Still, as any salesperson knows, it can be awfully easy to make the mistake of telling the customer what they want rather than waiting patiently for them to tell you. Sometimes, even experienced salespeople simply can't help themselves. Just as one of the tailors at Mitchells/Richards can size me up on first sight, twenty-five years of experience at a retail bike shop has taught me how to look at a customer and accurately gauge what size bike they might be considering. If you work at something forty to fifty hours every week like I do, that's about 2,000 hours a year or 50,000 hours over twenty-five years. With that many hours of practice, I've learned a few things along the way by default. As soon as I see a customer walk in the store, I run through the virtual database in my mind with everything I have in stock that might fit him or her—I just can't help myself. That's when I blink and remember what got us where we are today. I learned the hard way early in my career that making snap judgments about what *you think* customers want can really cost you in the long run.

• keep your focus •

I also always make the time to tell all my new employees about a hard lesson I learned back in 1982. I was eighteen at the time, scrambling around the shop, trying to do a hundred things at once. Then, one day, a customer walks in and tells me he's looking for a bike for his daughter, who would be heading off to college in a couple of weeks.

I immediately sized this guy up: he was wearing a dirty T-shirt and ripped shorts. He clearly had been working outdoors because his face was sunburned and his hair was sweaty and full of dust. I figured this guy didn't have much of a budget, so I picked out a decent $200 entry-level bike for him, telling him that it would do the trick. I spent all of ten minutes with the guy, hoping to get him out the door so that I could get back to the other stuff I was working on before he walked in. He was nice enough about it and, after paying me, he asked if I could give him a hand putting the bike in his car. I'm sure I was about to give him a look that said, "Are you kidding me?" but thought better of it and said, "No problem." Incidentally, I've come to realize the phrase "No problem" is as worthless as saying "Can I help you?" Why? Because the phrase discounts your customer's question, making it sound like it doesn't matter whether you care about the request or not. The proper response would have been "It would be my pleasure" or something of that sort to show that I both respected and wanted to please my new customer.

As I rolled the bike out to my customer's car, I learned a lesson in a big way. This guy was no ordinary customer; he drove a top-of-the-line Mercedes. "And all I sold him was a $200 bike?" I thought. When he saw me staring with my mouth open, he gave me a kind of knowing chuckle.

It turns out that this customer was actually an extremely successful business consultant who had been working on his sixty-foot yacht all day. He had noticed that I had an agenda and really hadn't taken the time to pay attention to him. Fortunately for me, he was extremely gracious about the whole experience. Rather than simply call me out for my mistake, he had asked me out to his car to teach me a lesson in dramatic fashion. He taught me how dangerous it can be to think that you know customers more than they know themselves.

Although I didn't do him a disservice with the bike I sold him, given that most bikes that get shipped off to college rarely make it back home afterward, my customer that day, who is now a longtime customer and friend, probably would have bought a $700 bike from me if I had really taken the time to connect with him. That was a time in my business life when every sale mattered. Missing the extra profit that higher-priced sale would have brought in made a difference in me making rent that month (meaning, I just barely scraped by); that's why I'll never forget that entire experience. It was an expensive lesson to learn—but one I am grateful for having learned so early.

 When you shrug off a compliment by a customer or a loved one, you are diminishing the value of that other person's words, devaluing words that he or she had carefully selected and presented to you as a gift.

That lesson also illustrates the importance of choosing your words carefully when interacting with your customers, your employees, and your loved ones as well. In our society, most of us don't know how to take a compliment anymore. We're also taught to be embarrassed when someone goes out of his or her way to thank us or point out something kind that we have done. Why have we forgotten to say simple things like *thank you* in response to praise? When you shrug off a compliment by a customer or a loved one, you are diminishing the value of that other person's words, devaluing words that he or she had carefully selected and presented to you as a gift.

As both a company and a culture, we need to get over any insecurity we might have about accepting compliments and recognize that they, like money, are payments made by our customers—invaluable praise bestowed by our customers in recognition of our hard work. This gets back to the point I made earlier about employees who go into autopilot mode and offer canned responses. When we fail to engage our customers—to thank them as well as accept their gratitude—we'll soon find ourselves out of business.

I end up telling the story about the guy in the Mercedes so often because it reinforces something else I learned from Tom Hopkins, the builder of sales champions, at a sales training conference in the mid-eighties. Tom's topic that day was about how, given that human beings have two ears and one mouth, we should be listening twice as much as we're talking. Thanks, Tom—if only I had seen your presentation earlier.

The key in selling is to guide customers toward what they really want. What *you* want them to do is irrelevant. That means that in order to sell effectively, you need to be asking questions to learn what your customer is looking for, not just turning on broadcast mode so you can tell them what you think they need.

As Tom likes to say in his lectures, "If the customer says it's true, then it's true. If you as the salesman say it, though, then the customer will doubt you." I've always found this to be profound advice and great insight into the mind of a consumer. Any time I, as a salesman, make a statement, a customer can challenge it.

As an example that touches on the importance of choosing your words carefully, think about what happens if I use the word *deal*, as in, "You might want to consider buying this bike because we have a deal running on it right now for a limited time only." Every word has a different meaning when it is used during the sales process, and the word *deal* begins to sound to customers like they're on the receiving end of a hard sell, that I'm now trying to ram something down their throats. That's why that word makes the hair on the back of their neck stand straight out. Not only does it put the customer on the defensive, but a *deal* means a cheap thing and it devalues the quality of our merchandise. We need to understand the psychological impact that our choice of words can have, which is why we should use the word *opportunity* instead because it is a positive word that speaks of promise and the future. Connecting with your customers is more than just choosing your words carefully; it's also about listening carefully to your customers' answers to put those opportunities in context.

The point is that I need to have the patience to ask my customer questions that might have nothing to do with the product itself at first. As soon as I give a customer the simple choice between a high-end $1,000 bike and a lower-end option that costs $350, that customer will almost always choose the latter option because I haven't asked them what they're looking for. If I first asked them about their riding conditions instead and learned that they do a lot of hill riding, I could point out that the $1,000 bike is a much lighter one with twenty-seven gears and would fly up and down mountains as compared to the twenty-one-geared bike that was both heavier and less refined. If I frame the choice in this context, the customer will say, "Well, I want the lighter bike, of course." Once I find the right question to ask customers, I can begin to steer them toward the option that will work best while avoiding wasting each other's time. In my experience, once a customer walks in the door, I have about twenty-five minutes to make some kind of connection with him or her. In other words, I don't have a second to waste.

An urban legend in the sales world suggests that the average customer's attention span is twenty-two minutes. Once the clock strikes that time, like Cinderella at midnight, every salesperson knows that the customer will head out the door, on his or her way toward becoming a pumpkin. But, because bikes and all their options are a fairly interesting topic to discuss—lots of gadgets!— I figure we have 10 percent more time—which is why we have twenty-five minutes to make that connection with the customer before giving up the cause.

Using those twenty-five minutes effectively is the challenge: if you talk too much, you leave less time to find out what makes your customer tick. You also have less time to find out what kind of experience he or she is looking for. When someone walks back out the door, the goal, of course, is to make sure that customer is leaving with whatever will best satisfy his or her needs.

• building relationships •

Although finding that piece of information that allows you to connect with a new customer can be challenging, we have other ways to make our existing customers feel like we're thinking about them all the time. The goal is not to make those customers feel like we're just trying to get into their wallets—we want them to feel a little better about their day because they took the time to drop by one of our stores. As you know by now, that's simply the business we're in. In the next chapter, we'll talk more about what it means to build a lifetime relationship with a customer.

· 2 ·

building lifetime relationships

A FEW YEARS after I took over my downtown Branford bike shop, I was invited out to Wisconsin for an industry trade show. This was a big thing for a young entrepreneur like me. I was at a national trade event—look at me! Little did I realize at the time what attending that show would actually mean to the maturation of my business. Although the main event was interesting and informative enough, it was actually a separate, hour-long breakout session I attended that had a profound effect on how I thought about my business.

The speaker was Dino Mancini, a trade show set designer who was working for Trek at the time.

Dino started his presentation by telling us that he was going to describe the kinds of adjectives normally associated with the kinds of images that would be displayed on the screen behind him. Using the words he chose, rather than by looking at the pictures he said would be displayed, he wanted us to guess what iconic brands he was describing through his words. He began by talking about crisp-looking blue and white shirts with pockets, khaki shorts, and denim pants— obviously things that made you think of The Gap and its casual clothing. Then he talked about vivid reds, yellows, and oranges; organic ingredients like lemon and avocado that make up fresh-smelling lotions and creams—things associated with The Body Shop. What about a blue box with a white ribbon tied neatly around it? A precious gift from Tiffany's, of course.

During all his descriptions, the screen behind Dino was blank. One guy even raised his hand halfway through and said, "Hey, your projector is broken." Dino kind of chuckled and replied, "You just missed the entire point." Dino's objective was to show how some brands can be identified just by describing the look, colors, and smells associated with them.

Like most of the attendees, I left his presentation scratching my head and thinking, "That was interesting, but I still don't get it!" During the next three weeks, the presentation continued to needle me. I just couldn't get the presentation out of my head. What the heck was Dino really driving at? I finally had my "Ah-ha!" moment, after which I figured out how I, too, could create that kind of visceral bond with my customers, so that if they closed their eyes, a certain kind of smell or image would immediately make them think of Zane's.

The answer I settled on was simple: a coffee bar. A few years earlier, I had taken a trip to Europe; one of my stops was a bike shop in Lucerne, Switzerland. The thing I'll never forget about that bike shop was its very cool coffee bar, where people relaxed, sipping their caffeinated drinks and talking about riding. I had never seen anything similar to that in the United States, so I figured I could do the same thing as that Swiss shop and really stand out with my customers.

I hired a guy who used to work for me in the bike shop to put together this fabulous-looking coffee and espresso bar. Today, I have customers coming in and telling me they love the smell of our store, which is really a mix of ground coffee and rubber. I know that might sound strange, but when you have 350 bikes on display—700 tires in all—that smell of new black tread makes a connection with people.

We combined this smell with visual effects as well—a black inlaid floor that resembles a black-topped road, complete with a double yellow line leading from the front door all the way back into the repair shop, as well as the kid's play area and our original sandbox (which I'll discuss more later). And behind the bar, we have a museum of sorts where we have hung all of the different Zane's signs and logos we have used over the years. Taking a seat at the bar, our customers can see the history of our branding development: our original stenciled sign, another one we call the

Adam Ant, our first professionally designed logo, as well as a gold-leaf, hand-carved marquee that helped build our image in the minds of our customers. They can compare our second logo, a picture of a guy riding a bike that used a spiral-like drawing style, and our current logo, the world-famous Zane's placard in bright orange. These additions have been so successful for us because they add to that image of our brand in our customers' heads—creating pictures and smells of what Zane's means, even when they have their eyes closed.

> Most bike shops don't have coffee bars, so that alone makes our shop stand out with customers. But, more important, the bar also serves as a connection point between our customers, something that allows them to slow down and enjoy being in the shop.

Of course, this is also the premise behind our newest Branford location: a distinctive building with the profile of a mountaintop, complete with a spinning bicycle-wheel (just like the one on the cover of this book) wind turbine on the roof. My goal is for all those folks traveling up and down I–95 to recognize our building—particularly because so many local media outlets have written so often about it. These changes are also intentionally designed to build a relaxed atmosphere where customers can turn off their defenses and enjoy themselves. After all, if we can find any other way to add to those twenty-five minutes that a customer might spend in our store, we'll take it.

Most bike shops don't have coffee bars, so that alone makes our shop stand out with customers. But, more important, the bar also serves as a connection point between our customers, something that allows them to slow down and enjoy being in the shop. I really do get a smile on my face every time I see a couple of customers strike up a conversation over coffee about an article one of them is reading about a particularly great ride. We also have customers who come in simply to grab a cup of joe so that they can tell us in detail about their latest ride. In other words, the bar helps us form a foundation for a lasting relationship with our customers, something that is far more valuable than most business owners realize. Having something that allows you to slow your customers' pace down is key because it gives you additional opportunities to find connection points with them. And, obviously, the more time someone spends in your shop, the greater the chance you have of selling him or her something.

Think about your daily trips to get gas, buy groceries, or drop off or pick up your dry cleaning; you want to get in and out as quickly as possible. That's why your grocer puts those free food samples at the end of the aisle—to get you to spend a few more minutes with them. Similarly, if you put cups of hot coffee in people's hands, they tend to slow down just to avoid spilling anything on themselves. More than that, our coffee bar becomes a way to show our customers that our store is fun to be in and they don't have to race through on their way back home. We brew an average of 150 pots of coffee a month in the off-season and up to 400 during the busy months, which, because we buy gourmet coffee, can cost anywhere from $150 to more than $300 a month.

But this isn't a cost for us—it's an investment. In that way, our bar also becomes a valuable staging ground for us on busy days. Rather than standing around twiddling their thumbs, waiting customers can have something to drink, read a magazine, or look at trail maps of local rides while we finish up with our other customers. Also, customers actually feel better on a coffee high and are much more likely to buy. Rather than looking for someplace to sit and relax, they're all amped up, ready to take a test ride and actively participate in the exciting process of selecting their new bikes. I even remember one customer who, pre-coffee, was hemming and hawing over whether to plunk down his wallet to buy a new bike. But, after a nice hot fresh cup of coffee, he ended up buying not one but two bikes. Coffee also serves as a great way to keep *my employees* in the shop: rather than worrying about whether one of them will be down the street at the coffee shop when a customer comes in, I know that by having a great offering of coffee, both my employees and customers will be satisfying their cravings nose to nose. A cup of coffee could actually offer an immediate way for my salespeople to make that first connection with a thirsty or undercaffeinated customer. In other words, the bar helps us keep our customers happy, even when we're a bit too tied up to give them one-on-one attention. That's a hugely valuable fact that goes a long way toward winning the long-term loyalty of those customers.

I also took another lesson from Dino Mancini's presentation and started wrapping our customers' purchases in brown craft paper tied up with a ribbon with the Zane's logo printed on it—to make us, in essence, the Tiffany's of the bike business. We also have been creative when it comes to the packaging of our gift certificates. Most gift certificates I receive come in boring white envelopes. Our gift certificates come in water bottles with *Zane's* printed on them. Sure, I might have been able to sell those bottles for five dollars apiece, but think about the impact I get instead. Why on earth would one of our customers ever go buy from a competitor after getting more service or being treated better than they expected, let alone to a place that still puts their gift certificates in plain white envelopes? The beauty of this principle is that it has nothing to do with bike shops: you could be selling any product or service. It works if you run a bank, a salon, or a snowplowing business like the one run by the friends I mentioned previously. Whenever a business delivers more than someone expects, it will be rewarded sooner or later. The key is to do it in a way that pokes your customers in the ribs a bit, that reminds them you just did something that you didn't have to and shows you're ready to keep doing it time and time again.

• the lifetime value of customers •

A huge component in building a lasting relationship with a customer is to find a way to establish enough trust so that he or she feels that we're not just there to soak them out of every dollar we can. After all, they've been conditioned to resist the hard sell based on their interactions with everyone from auto dealers to real estate agents. If you can shift your thinking away from merely selling and into building some trust instead, even if it costs you a few bucks in profit, you'll begin to see opportunities you never imagined. It starts when you understand what it means to "wow" that customer by giving him or her more than expected. When we started adjusting our thinking about our customers so that we began to consider the lifetime value of their business—that is $12,500 in our case—we could shift our thinking to what we were willing to spend to turn all those one-time purchases into lifetime customers. Any business that isn't thinking along these lines is simply playing in the wrong game.

Tropicana, for example, is one of our partners on the commercial side of our business. The folks who work at the kingpin of orange juice told me that the lifetime value of one of their customers is $32,500. They arrived at that figure by estimating that the average customer will buy somewhere in the neighborhood of six thousand cartons of their juice over time. No wonder the company's marketing efforts are focused on children, right? On the other hand, the lifetime customer value to the owner of your neighborhood pizza joint is $25,000. That's a lot of pizza—and once that owner starts thinking about his or her customers as having more value than the $20 pepperoni special they just ordered, the more successful the owner can be.

Saying that you want to create a lifetime relationship with your customers is one thing; it's quite another to make it happen. To be successful at building these kinds of relationships often requires you to think differently about why your customer needs you in the first place. In this virtual age, where so many transactions happen with no human being involved, finding a way to make emotional connections with your customers is key.

> In this virtual age, where so many transactions happen with no human being involved, finding a way to make emotional connections with your customers is key.

For example, the Internet has made travel agents extinct for the most part. Who wants to pay someone else a nice fee when he or she can plan a trip right from the computer, right? I have to admit that I also thought this way until I had the chance to talk to a friend who worked as a travel agent for many years. He reminded me that the real value he gave his customers was when their flight was canceled or when a hotel couldn't find their reservation. In other words, my friend proved his value to his customer when the poop hit the fan, so to speak. If he could bail his customers out of troublesome and emotional situations such as rebooking a family on another flight or finding them a new hotel down the road, those customers would often be so thankful they would never think about booking another trip without my friend's help.

I realized that this same principle applies to buying bikes: anyone can go online and shop for a bike. You can even get a lot of great advice about what kind of bike and parts you need if you keep up with the industry blogs and online user discussion forums. If you looked at all the odds stacked against you as a retail bike shop, why would you have any confidence whatsoever that anyone would actually make the effort of stopping by our store to buy a bike? The answer, we came to realize, was because we would be there when one of our customers' children's bikes breaks or, to move up the food chain, when the parent of a child who rides one of our bikes needs to find a replacement part in a pinch. In other words, we want our customers to come in and buy from us because we will take care of their needs far better than any retailer who thinks of them simply as an e-mailed order number.

Our goal is to show our customers that we want each of them to feel as if they can always rely on us, especially after they've left our store with their new bikes. We also want to emphasize that when they do come back to us for help, we see those visits as opportunities to further our relationship with them, not just additional chances to ring up another dollar on the cash register.

• the end of nickel-and-diming •

While we embark on this grand new adventure of opening a chain of national bike shops, I can also look back at my history of involvement in businesses of all kinds, beginning with my first paper route. I can now see something of a serial entrepreneur in my nature. That means, perhaps, that I get bored without some new challenges to tackle. That's why in addition to running my Branford shop, I was a partner in a local liquor store for a few years. But I didn't do this as a lark. I often used my time running the register there to experiment with ways to keep customers coming back to pick up their six-packs of beer or bottles of wine. It was here, actually, that I came upon a key realization that has influenced my actions to this day: most customers sleepwalk through their decisions. By that, I mean all of us make decisions without really thinking about where we want to get gas, dry cleaning, or a six-pack for the weekend.

Once I understood this, I wanted to find ways to wake people up, so to speak, and implant something in their subconscious, so that next time they have a buying decision to make, they'll already be thinking of me. One of the strategies I used was to wait until customers had walked out to their cars and then run out the door after them. I would tell them that I had accidentally given them the wrong change and would then hand over a crisp one dollar bill, reimbursing them for my error (all the time knowing I had done no such thing). Customers would often look at me in amazement and appreciation for the effort. And you can bet that they knew where to go the next time they needed to visit a liquor store. Of course, on my end, I only earned one dollar of profit on a six-pack, so I was actually handing over my entire profit in order to build a longer-term relationship with that customer. I found that investment paid for itself time and time again.

I owe my own understanding of this idea—that customers need to be prodded from time to time—to a mortgage broker who gave a speech on this topic during a networking dinner I attended a few years ago. Not unlike my travel agent friend, this mortgage broker talked about how, in giving out customer satisfaction surveys, she learned an extraordinary thing: that the harder it was for a customer to secure a loan, the higher their satisfaction level with the broker. The reason for this seemingly counterintuitive notion, she told us, was that the people who almost didn't get their mortgage saw how hard their broker was working to help them. Because the broker and the customer were in almost constant contact, reviewing pay stubs, calling up banks, or checking references, the customer understood how difficult the entire process was. Customers with perfect credit scores and plenty of money for down payments, on the other hand, ranked their satisfaction levels lower simply because they didn't need to see how hard their broker was working for them. I was fascinated by this realization that part of providing great service is reminding your customer how hard you're working to deliver that service, to make their lives easier. And, of course, providing a key service at a time when your customer is feeling the most pain is one surefire way for them to understand and acknowledge what you've done.

When it came to the bike shop, I adapted the strategy from our liquor store experiments somewhat. One of the ways that we have gone about building a sense of trust with our customers is that we have stopped charging our customers for anything that costs us less than one dollar. That means that we'll give away parts like ball bearings, master links (part of a bike's chain), and various nuts and bolts for which we used to charge $1.99 apiece—which our competitors still do. Part of this strategy is built upon the recognition that most of the opportunities to give these parts away come during painful times for our customer. For instance, when a father comes into the store, looking somewhat worn out because his kid is in the car crying about the broken chain on his bike, we'll just hand that dad a free master link to fix it. Matter of fact, we'll give him two, in case he needs another replacement down the road. We do this because it lets our customers know we're not out to milk them—we're there to save them the hassle and the expense of getting their kids back out on the street and riding their bikes. We want them to know we're not just here to take, and that we're willing to go the extra mile to make them feel special—a key component of helping them to think of themselves as lifetime customers. When you look at the benefits to this program, I'd be willing to eat a lot of extra master links. But, when we added up what this strategy was costing us, it made my one-dollar giveaways on six-packs look foolish.

We actually tracked the costs of our giveaways one year and, incredibly, it came to just about eighty-six dollars. Breaking it down further, that eighty-six dollars bought us about 450 one-on-one interactions with various customers, most of whom were in some form of distress when we handed over the part they needed. Think about that: for eighty-six dollars, we got back 450 chances to alleviate a bit of pain for our customers and create a lasting memory while doing it. Compare the value of all that goodwill we created with the thousands of dollars it would have cost to rent a billboard or place an ad in the local paper. It's kind of like that credit card commercial: one ball bearing—five cents. A happy customer who keeps coming back because you've just made his or her life a little bit easier—priceless.

• life is like a bowl of quarters •

Somewhere along the road in my twenty-five years in the business, I stumbled across a great way to illustrate how much I'm willing to dole out to my customers with the goal of turning them into lifetime customers. My secret sauce? A bowl of quarters.

Imagine you're in the audience when I'm giving a talk about the lifetime value of customers. The first thing that I explain is that, because I'm in the service business and everyone knows service costs money, I'm prepared to spend some on that audience right then and there. That's when I dig out my bowl of quarters, about $100 worth. To me, that bowl hypothetically represents how much I'm willing to spend on any one customer in the form of service, attention, or some other form of extraordinary effort that leads to creating a unique customer experience. Some people in the audience chuckle while others get this quizzical look on their faces as I next take a quick spin around the room and present a half dozen or so folks with the bowl, inviting them to help themselves. Some people take a single quarter; others take a bunch. I've done this more than a hundred times, in venues all over the world, and no one has ever taken the whole bowl. (I'm still waiting for the first.)

The point is that when you as a customer are presented with more than what seems reasonable, like a bowl of 400 quarters, you will self-regulate. To hammer this point home further, I then walk around the audience again and give out a few more quarters to the attendees who were originally offered the bowl, explaining, "At Zane's Cycles, we offer more service than what seems reasonable." By providing more service and attention than most folks consider reasonable—like giving away any parts that cost us less than one dollar—we build trust and loyalty with our customers and remind them how hard we're working on their behalf.

By providing more service and attention than most folks consider reasonable—like giving away any parts that cost us less than one dollar—we build trust and loyalty with our customers and remind them how hard we're working on their behalf.

As hard as it is to win a customer's loyalty, and regardless of how big your bowl of quarters is, you can also lose that customer in a heartbeat if you and your employees ever turn on your autopilot. I was reminded of this at another sales conference I attended, when I heard Dave Mitchell, who talked about how Disney Corporation related to its customers in their hotel business. As a visual, Dave created a kind of speedometer with his arm to show that a customer's satisfaction level is neutral before they arrive at the hotel. But as soon as he or she pulls up to the entrance, the customer's meter begins to climb or fall, depending on the condition of the entryway, the lobby, and the friendliness of the staff behind the counter.

At some point, though, Dave explained, that meter will begin to settle on either the positive or the negative side of neutral, almost like it is made of wet concrete that is beginning to harden. That means that the hotel staff has a fixed amount of time to get that meter on the positive side because once the customer steps inside his or her room, the concrete meter will be set. That's why the nicest part of any hotel is its lobby—it's a conscious effort on the part of the hotel to get that meter climbing as soon as that customer walks in. But keeping that meter climbing takes an increasing amount of energy, and more and more quarters to keep it pointed upwards. That also means that it becomes that much easier to lose that customer if you don't have your bowl to fall back on.

The single biggest factor in driving down a customer's meter, the speaker said, was when he or she gets to the room and the key doesn't work. At that point, no matter how much energy you've expended to build a positive image for that customer, you basically have to begin from scratch or, worse, from a negative position in hardened concrete.

I like this visualization of the process of winning over customers because it makes sense. It's just so much harder to move that customer's perception of your business if you haven't started off on the positive end of the meter. And once the concrete around that meter sets, you can almost pack your bags because it will cost you more than just a bowl of quarters to win that customer back. But, if you can ever help customers during a time of pain and remind them of how hard you're working on their behalf, well, you can magically soften that concrete a bit and start that meter moving again.

Think about the story of the snowplow company who brought the trashcans in for its customers. By finding a way to remind its customers of what it was doing, like putting stickers on the cans, those guys could move their customers' meters forward a bit. The same concept applies when I walk into my neighborhood coffee shop and they tell me I'll have to wait ten minutes while they brew another pot. As soon as I hear that, my personal meter takes a big dip as I sigh and think about all the things I need to do. "I'm never coming back here again," I might say to myself. "The last thing I want to do is wait for my coffee!" But when the person behind the counter tells me, "Sorry for the wait; this coffee is on us today," well, my meter suddenly springs to life and takes a nice big uptick.

I like to tell people what Gary Loveman has done at Harrah's in Las Vegas to show how other businesses have adopted similar programs. I attend four or five trade shows in Las Vegas each year, and I'll always stay at Caesars Palace (the nicest of Harrah's properties) because I'm both familiar with it and because they send me rewards promotions based on how much I've spent on my prior visits. I might get a free night's stay or a chit for fifty dollars just to remind me that Caesars appreciates my business. But under Gary's direction, the casino goes even further. The days of the coin-slot machines are long gone. Today, everything works via a special loyalty or players card, which you can use for buying everything from poker chips to potato chips. But that card is also useful for the casino to keep its eyes on you. There is actually a room full of pit bosses that monitor what you're spending, how much you're betting, and even if you're on a tough losing streak.

Gary understands that losing streaks are bad things, especially for first-time customers. So, as soon as his team sees a new customer start losing—just visualize that satisfaction meter starting to point straight down—they'll send someone down to him or her with an extra fifty dollars or a meal coupon to turn that meter right around. Gary knows he has a chance to change that customer's attitude before the mortar sets and he's got a big bowl of quarters to dip into to make that happen.

One key aspect that the speaker talking about Disney missed in his presentation and something that Gary understands well is the value of a customer's meter over the lifetime of your relationship with him or her. The key is not to think about that meter in terms of a single transaction but as part of a lasting sequence of events. When you start looking for clues for how the best-run companies in the world think about this sequence you'll notice that these companies understand the value of return customers, so they're willing to pay to keep you coming back as a customer again and again. If I haven't visited Jack Mitchell's store in a few months, for example, I get a personalized coupon for $100 in the mail, letting me know that they missed me. Staples does the same thing when I haven't been back to stock up on office supplies for a while. We do something similar with the help of our computerized customer database. From the very beginning of computerized point of sale systems, I have been a disciple of keeping everything from my inventory to purchase records on computers. As a result, I now have about twenty years of customer histories to turn to for help in continuing or even starting a conversation with our customers.

Let me explain how this works before you start thinking we are running some sort of Big Brother operation. Let's say that we have a return customer who walks into our shop after work. Rather than starting our conversation from scratch, the salesperson can ask for her name and quickly look up her purchase history with us. That's when the salesperson notices that she stops into the shop every six months or so; each time she does, she picks up a new piece of gear like a pump or a helmet. Bingo—those are the seeds to begin a conversation. Rather than wasting a whole lot of time talking about what our customer has already bought, we can then spend our time talking about what kind of gear she might be looking for this time. Remember, we only have that customer's attention for twenty-five minutes, so time's a-wasting.

Along those same lines, we also use the information in our database to send customized flyers to our customers, letting them know of a special event, for example, when we have an opportunity to purchase a specific size, let's say men's medium, of some popular clothing on closeout. We send out an e-mail blast or postcard, letting all of our male customers who have ever bought a piece of medium-sized clothing that we are having a sale (not mentioning specifically medium, but just a sale on shorts). When he arrives, wow, there's a sale rack full of clothes in his size, how lucky is he. We can use that information as a predictive tool as well. If we sell a 16-inch bike to the parents of a five-year-old, we can bet that same family will be ready to upgrade to a 20-inch bike in another two years. The same goes for a high-end customer. She might have bought our lightest bike five years ago, but now that Trek has introduced its even lighter version, we'll send her a note to let her know all about it. Along with it is a reminder to stop in for free servicing of her existing bike, coaxing her into the store. The goal, of course, is to let that customer know that we're thinking about her. And, rather than making nuisances of ourselves, we're also trying to anticipate how we might make a lasting impression with her in a very personal way by homing in on the kinds of things she likes best.

Of course, we also have to walk a fine line in our efforts to personalize those one-on-one customer relationships. We have to be conscious of how we use this customer data; we would never want to tip the scales and use it in any kind of creepy manner. Plus, the last thing we want to do is offend any of our customers by sending information revealing how singularly focused we are on them; God forbid someone has lost or gained weight since the last time they've bought something. Sometimes, I suppose, there can be too much of a personal relationship with your customers; we need to be sensitive about their privacy.

One cautionary tale I heard on this very subject happened to a high-end jewelry store that will remain unnamed. This store, like us, kept track of all of its customers' purchases over the years. One year, to kick off a big holiday sales push, the store sent out invitations by mail to all of its high-end customers—those folks who had spent a lot of money on expensive jewelry in the past. In the mailer, which was sent directly to the customers' home addresses, the store had printed something like, "To our high-priced jewelry customers . . ."

On the face of it, this may seem like a very reasonable marketing effort. Unfortunately for the store, though, it was a gigantic disaster. It turns out that not all that expensive jewelry was ever making it back home to whomever was opening the mail that day. I guess there were plenty of husbands with secretaries wearing some pricey jewelry who returned home to more than a few rude awakenings that night.

• don't just talk the talk, walk the walk •

As a teenager, I remember buying a book by Joe Karbo called *A Lazy Man's Ways to Riches*. But this was no ordinary book. The interesting thing was that if you bought Joe's book, you could mail it back to him within thirty days and he would refund the cost of the book. To make his point, Joe had included a letter in each book that said the reason he was rich and I, the reader, wasn't, was because he predicted that I would be too lazy to return the book and get my money back. But Joe didn't stop there. He challenged his readers that if we, too, wanted to become rich like him, we should read the entire book, make sense of all the valuable information he shared in it, and then simply return it for a full refund. In other words, Joe was actually goading his customers to take advantage of his offer.

Guess what? That book is still on my bookshelf. Although I still think Joe's book has some great advice about goal setting, the takeaway point from this story is that most people won't take full advantage of every deal they come across (even if you goad them). At the same time, Joe was prepared to buy back every single one of his books if his customers pushed him to—just like we at Zane's need to be prepared to tip over our bowl of quarters when a customer asks us to.

Granted, it's not always easy to think this way. It's only human nature to push back from time to time when you feel like a customer is asking for too much. That's why we're constantly reinforcing the notion that we need to think about the lifetime value of our customers to help put the little things in perspective.

I remember a recent case where a man, a doctor in fact, came into the store to return a bike tube. It clearly had a hole created by a screwdriver in it—he must have slipped and accidentally punctured the new tube when he was changing his tube. But rather than own up to it, our customer insisted that we had sold him a defective tube. I watched as my employee who was waiting on the customer began to get a bit riled up. "Sir, there's no possible way we sold you this part in this condition," he said. Although I couldn't have agreed more, I walked over to the shelf, grabbed a new tube, and made a brief detour to the coffee bar for a cup of hot coffee. I then handed both over to the customer and thanked him for bringing the defective tube to our attention. The doc kind of looked at me strangely at first, but after a sip of coffee, I could see him visibly relax. He even smiled—not the smile of a huckster but a smile that said, "Wow, thanks."

After the doctor left, my employee came up to me to ask why I had given in to a customer who was clearly trying to take advantage of us. "Look," I said. "That guy could come back in here tomorrow and buy a $2,000 bike from us—and some of the profits of that will go directly to you. When you look at it like that, a six-dollar tube is not even worth a conversation." That tube serves as a small but critical lesson that all my employees should remember, especially as we continue to expand nationally. We should always be prepared to let a customer reach into that bowl of quarters, confident we can land that customer for life.

I like to share another story along the same lines with my employees; it stars a female customer who once made it clear she was going to put our policies to the test. One day, this woman walked into the shop, rolling her bike along with her. She immediately told us that she wanted to trade in her bike so she could purchase another. "Ah, sorry," I told her. "We don't take trade-ins."

"Fine, then I want to return it," she said, as she began reciting our policy covering returns back to me exactly line for line. "*You will, without reservation, guarantee that if for any reason, at any time, I am not completely satisfied with any item I purchased from you, you will gladly repair, replace, or refund my money.* Well, I'm not satisfied with my bike, so I'd like a refund," she said in a now-less-than-friendly way. I was then faced with a dilemma: I could easily press the point that it took her an entire *six years* of riding her bike to figure out that she wasn't satisfied with it. Or, I could just eat the cost of her bike and let her pick another.

In truth, there was never really any choice in the matter. As soon as I start to make exceptions to our rules, Zane's would soon find itself in trouble. "Okay," I said, immediately creating a transaction to refund her the total cost of the bike along with all the installed accessories. She said I could just issue her a credit, but I wanted to send her the message, as well as my staff, that by crediting her credit card for the full amount, moving forward on her next purchase wasn't required in order for us to live up to our service offering. "Now, let's see if we can pick something else out that you'll like better."

I was fully expecting her to pick out a bike about equal in value to her old bike, which we had sold to her for $480. Because we don't sell used bikes, all I could see was red ink: we were going to be left with a used bike that we couldn't do anything with, plus we'd be out the price of a new bike. Fortunately for us, our customer had her eyes on a bigger prize. Just as she had done her homework on our return policy, she had apparently done an equal amount of research into her choice for a new cycle. She actually picked out a $1,200 bike—for which she happily doled out $700 more than we credited her for her old bike. Although we didn't make the kind of margin I would have liked on that bike, taking the return into consideration, we still turned a profit on the transactions and, more importantly, we continued the love affair with a cycling enthusiast who we trusted would be stopping back at the shop soon to pick up lots of high-profit-margin accessories. Looking back on interactions with this customer, she's probably the only customer who truly dipped into the bowl of quarters, having tipped the entire thing into her purse. But the point of the story is that we should be willing to do just that for all of our customers. The real dividend from that whole experience was that it sparked some creative juices in my staff, which led to us implementing one of the most successful programs we've ever launched within our retail business, a program that continues to pay dividends even today.

• trade in, trade up •

Coming on the heels of that customer who pushed our return policy to its limits, Tom, our director of retail operations, recognized that we were losing an increasing number of our kids' bike sales to Walmart. Of course, this made perfect sense because Walmart was charging sixty-nine dollars for 12- and 16-inch bikes, about half the price we were charging for a very similar-looking bike. But we didn't set our prices artificially high. Our bikes are made of better and stronger components; in addition, we assemble our bikes for our customers. We were actually selling a superior bike to those available from Walmart's shelves and we needed to set a price that reflected the extra attention we put into our bikes. There was no way we wanted to cut our price closer to sixty-nine dollars and find ourselves involved in a price war we could never win.

Fortunately for Zane's, we had Tom on our side. Not only is Tom one of the best store managers I've ever met, I'm pretty sure he walks on water and glows in the dark. After watching what was happening with the Walmart situation, Tom recognized that our customers, who were parents, might want to save a few bucks on their kids' first or second bikes. After all, their kids were probably going to grow out of whatever bike they bought within a year or two anyway.

That's where Tom's inspiration came in. He launched a program where he told parents that once their children outgrew their bikes, they could simply bring their bikes back to the shop and trade them in for a full credit toward the purchase of a new bike. That meant those parents could apply the $129 they paid two years ago to purchase that 12-inch bike toward buying a new 16-inch model. And it didn't end there; once the kids hit their growth spurt, they could trade that 16-inch bike in for a 20-inch model. As a parent, there was virtually no downside to this program. As soon as word started getting out that we were doing this, our sales of kids' bikes went through their own impressive growth spurt.

I have to admit that when Tom first told me about the program, I started to sweat a little. All I could see were rows and rows filled with thousands of returned children's bikes we'd be stuck with. Tom dismissed me as coolly as a cucumber. "Chris," he said as he put his arm around my shoulder. "Think about it. Every bike we sell is potentially building a new lifetime relationship both with the kid and with his or her parents. Sure, we'll end up with some returned bikes, but we can donate those to other kids in the area who can't afford to get bikes as good as ours. Meanwhile, we have these parents practically lining up around the corner to get in here and spend their money." The point, he reminded me, was that we had a chance to keep those kids and their parents coming back to the store for years—the same mantra I had been trying to preach to him for years. Ah, I finally realized, here is someone who gets what Zane's Cycles is all about.

The surprise ending to this story was that, although I was prepared to make good on the whole bowl of quarters all those returns would add up to, only about 20 percent of the people who bought the bikes ever brought them back. At first, we were baffled. "What's going on?" we wondered. I was worried that if no one took advantage of the program, it would seem like we were promoting something that no one was interested in. We even began calling up our customers just to remind them that they were about due to trade in their kids' bikes for upgrades.

The funny thing was that when we started talking to these customers about why they hadn't returned to trade in their old bikes, most of them told us they simply didn't want to. Most of the folks we talked to said they had other younger children or relatives who had already inherited the bikes. Because our bikes were virtually indestructible, parents saw no good reason to turn them back in. When we started looking at the program in this light, we realized that not only had we boosted our sales, without discounting them, for our kids' bikes, we also helped our customers recognize the quality of our bikes. This program has become so popular that I even have my own kids' friends coming over to the house to tell me how cool it is. Think these kids will remember Zane's when it comes time for them to buy bikes for their own kids? Talk about a lifetime relationship!

> Besides helping us build lifetime relationships with our customers, our trade-in program continues to generate an enormous amount of positive buzz for Zane's.

• guerilla marketing •

Besides helping us build lifetime relationships with our customers, our trade-in program continues to generate an enormous amount of positive buzz for Zane's. We certainly feel good about ourselves when we donate dozens of slightly used but top-quality bikes to underprivileged kids every six months or so. But there are secondary benefits to this program as well. For instance, we get a lot of attention from the local media, not only for the trade-ins, but for our other innovative customer service programs. When a parent or cyclist who shops with my competitors reads about all the great things we're doing for our customers, it doesn't take long for them to decide to drop by and see for themselves what we're up to. (Talk about guerilla marketing—we basically encourage the local media to advertise for us!) In the next chapter, we'll talk more about how the idea of creating an unbeatable value proposition can be one of the best marketing tools around.

· 3 ·

a winning proposition

WHEN IT COMES to marketing a business and building a brand, the goal should be promoting how that business is different from every other business out there. The one program that is most connected with the Zane's brand has to be our lifetime service guarantee. That means that anyone who buys a bike from us can bring that bike back in for any needed tune-ups and repairs that result from everyday riding wear and tear for the entire life of the bike. When we started the program back in 1995, opinion was split about it: our customers absolutely fell in love with it although my competitors and other supposed experts were convinced it was going to lead me into bankruptcy.

It was Donna Fenn of *Inc.* who really stoked our critics when she wrote about some of the innovative programs we were running at Zane's, like our service guarantee, in the February 1996 issue of the magazine. After the article, which ran with the headline "Leader of the Pack," came out, it seemed like everyone and their mother was writing letters to the industry trade journals talking about how crazy I was to be giving things away for free. Obviously, they had never heard me talk about my bowl of quarters and how much I'm willing to spend on folks walking into our shop to turn them into lifetime customers. Eventually, my competitors began to realize that not only was I not going out of business because of my programs, I was actually growing my sales 25 percent a year by stealing *their* customers. It turns out that I have had the last laugh. Of course, not everything happened overnight—particularly our commitment to lifetime free service.

• the lifetime service guarantee •

When I took over ownership of my bike shop back in 1981, most of my time was spent assembling and repairing bikes. Ever since I was a kid, I've been mechanically inclined and had a fondness for working with my hands, so tinkering with tools, gears, sprockets, and other parts has always come naturally to me. I also pride myself on doing things the right way to ensure that we head off future problems, which means doing a repair or a build only once whenever I can help it. And that's the kind of attitude we embrace as an organization.

One of the first things you do in assembling a bike that has been shipped by a manufacturer, for example, is to slide the steel brake cable through the bike's housing frame. The problem with that steel cable is that it tends to rust over time, especially if the bike's owner does a lot of off-road riding or leaves the bike out in the rain. That's why when a Zane's mechanic assembles a bike, we now coat that cable in some grease. That means that no matter what happens to that bike or even what kinds of conditions it is ridden in, that cable is not going to rust.

Although this might seem like a minor detail, it is precisely the kind of detail that allows us to engage in aggressive guerilla marketing efforts like our lifetime service guarantee, a program that actually has its roots as a one-year free service program (covering parts and labor on all routine service) that I first used to distinguish myself from my seventeen competitors.

Because I was doing most of the assembly and repair work myself in the beginning, I knew I was doing quality work. If I focused on the high-impact details, like greasing a brake cable or tightening a loose spoke, I could keep my bikes running longer and more safely than those put together by my competitors—most of whom saw the opportunity to make some extra money from their customers by charging for repair jobs that could have been avoided by some simple preventative maintenance. The difference was that the mechanics who worked for my competitors generally earned their pay as nonsalaried contractors, which meant they got paid a commission fee on each repair they completed. This is the kind of business model many people seem to think auto mechanics and dealerships use. In other words, these mechanics had a strong incentive to create as many problems as possible so that they could make money rather than do the necessary preventative work that would keep a bike from ever coming back into the shop.

If something did go wrong with one of my bikes, I wanted to make good on it. As a matter of fact, it became a point of pride for me and my mechanics to make sure we did the job correctly, so that we never saw that bike back in the shop again. That's why I knew that offering a one-year free service guarantee wouldn't actually cost me much because I knew most of the bikes wouldn't need any work. But the real advantage of this program was that I was establishing a relationship with my customers where they could trust that I wasn't trying to milk them for the price of extra parts or service trips—when they bought a bike from Zane's, they knew it would be built as well and as safely as we could do it.

> My competitors didn't understand that I had changed the rules of the game on them and that every time they thought they were matching me, they were actually falling further behind.

Over the following years, as my competitors saw that they were losing their customers to me, they, too, began offering one-year service guarantees. The truth was they didn't understand that I had changed the rules of the game on them and that every time they thought they were matching me, they were actually falling further behind.

By the time my competitors grasped that they were losing their customers to me in part because of my service guarantee, I had already had about a year's worth of experience of working under the program—which gave me invaluable insight and confidence in understanding how offering free service didn't mean I was giving away the store. From the beginning, I tracked every repair job in our computer system and I knew that a very small percentage of the bikes we built ever came back for servicing. So, as my competitors began promoting their one-year service guarantee programs, I felt there was very little risk in trumping my competitors by offering a two-year service guarantee. I knew that I could simply chalk up the extra repair costs to losing a few quarters toward the $12,500 I wanted to win over time.

But the game soon changed permanently. I was attending a trade show where someone was touting their company's products' lifetime guarantee when it hit me: why don't we just offer lifetime free service, too? By this point, I had about five years' worth of data that showed that we still had just a small percentage of our bikes getting returned for service. There was no real difference on our end between the two-year guarantee and a lifetime guarantee—but it could mean all the difference in cementing a lifetime relationship with a customer. (I also knew it would really knock the socks off my competitors, one of those rare win-win-win scenarios.)

To this day, we offer our lifetime service guarantee, which by the way, we made retroactive on all the bikes we have ever sold. We want our customers to know that, by buying from us, they are buying more than just a bunch of parts bolted together; they're buying a relationship with us where we're going to treat them right.

My competitors, on the other hand, have always approached the game backward. They saw our "guarantee arms race" simply as a marketing gimmick, not grasping that their entire business would collapse like a house of cards as soon as they began offering their own lifetime free service. For one, as soon the shop owner starting offering free service, they would have to work something out with their mechanics about how they would get paid for their work. This meant dissension in the ranks—and some sleepless nights for my competitors—which worked beautifully for me in terms of trying to recruit away the most talented mechanics.

The real problem for my competition, though, was that as soon as one of these shops began offering a free service guarantee, they were opening themselves up to a massive liability, namely that it was possible that they would be swamped with service calls on every bike they had sold or repaired over the past years because their business model had always been based on making money off return service visits. When my competitors thought about generating revenue, they loved the idea of making it on service, which they considered to be close to 100 percent profit, rather than on selling bikes or merchandise, which have more like 45 percent profit margins.

Now, by introducing free service guarantees, they were faced with a serious problem because the whole system they had rigged to ensure that they received plenty of profitable repeat service calls was collapsing around them. The shops were busier than they ever were, but they weren't making any money. Unlike me and my mechanics, who have always been focused on building our bikes correctly the first time so that our customer wouldn't have to bring them back, my competitors soon found themselves bleeding to death trying to keep up with us. As a matter of fact, it wasn't long before the reputation of our mechanics and their ability to repair bikes so they stayed working correctly had my competitors' customers coming to us for repairs. That meant these customers were so unhappy with the service they received at the shop they bought their bikes from, they would rather pay Zane's to fix their bikes than have the original shop do it for free. As you could imagine, it didn't take long under these conditions before most of my immediate competitors were forced to go out of business.

• offer the best value package •

Despite our success at both pleasing our customers and putting our competitors out of business, I still get people who come up to me and say that we're insane for offering our lifetime free service guarantee. But, in my opinion, any business owner who doesn't explore the concept in his or her own way is the crazy one. Again, it took me several years of operating the business before I built up enough confidence to take the leap to a lifetime guarantee. But when I made the leap, I knew I had the facts on my side: if we did our jobs correctly right off the bat, there was actually zero downside to guaranteeing our work. Because I paid my mechanics a salary rather than a commission, they had all the incentive in the world not to work on the same bike more than once if they could help it. They get paid the same, so why would they want to do the same thing more than once? In fact, I'd be close to nirvana if my mechanics had so little work to do they could just sit around and drink coffee with my customers and talk about their most recent ride. After all, we are in the business of selling experiences, not parts and repair jobs.

Our goal has always been to blow our customers away by offering them the best value package on the market—not simply to try to dig deeper into their wallets. Because service is free (not to mention the coffee), there is no penalty or expense to the customer if they just keep bringing it back until it's right. But, because of our focus on doing things the right way the first time, our mechanics began to attract new customers who had become dissatisfied by the service they received elsewhere—even if it was free. Seeing customers behave this way got me to thinking that we had hit upon a new way to hold on to our existing customers and break through all the marketing noise out there to attract new customers who saw extra value in the kind of quality service we provided.

This idea really hit home for me during a presentation I attended by Brad Edmundson of *American Demographics* magazine in the mid-'90s. Brad was discussing the results of a survey that broke down consumers into three groups based on their buying habits and price sensitivity. The results showed that some 30 percent of customers ultimately make their buying decisions based solely on price. These are the kinds of people that will drive 100 miles just to save five dollars on a purchase—not my preferred customer. The second group of customers, another 30 percent, will make their decisions based on the best service. These are the folks that make purchasing decisions based on quality and service, regardless of price. The most interesting result for me was that the remaining 40 percent of buyers could be swayed either by the promise of low prices or by the promise of superior quality and service, depending on which message was the most convincing.

That blew me away because it completely simplified how we could approach the marketing of our business. We already knew we would win over those 30 percent of customers who would be swayed by top-notch service. But rather than waste our time marketing to that other 30 percent of customers who were bent on finding the best price, we could dedicate ourselves to swaying those 40 percent of customers sitting on the fence by offering the best value package anywhere on the market. In other words, we could try to create a plan with multiple messages and hope to attract

100 percent of the market but ultimately capturing only 50 percent of the customers due to an inconsistent brand message, or we could create a single message specific to 40 percent of the market and capture 70 percent of the customers.

Although that goal sounded reasonable enough, we weren't sure where to begin. What could we do to enhance our value proposition beyond lifetime free service? We eventually arrived at our answer after we began analyzing the kinds of service our customers were bringing their bikes in for. The vast majority of the time, it was something like a derailleur breaks on the road or the trail—something that we aren't at fault for—and it breaks because the rider takes a spill or lands on a rock or something. Normally, we would replace the part and ship the broken one back to the manufacturer. Sometimes, we might even receive a credit back from our vendor if the part turned out to be defective in some way. But, as we dug deeper into this situation, we had a revelation of sorts: why couldn't we also offer a lifetime parts warranty in addition to our lifetime service guarantee? (To clear up any confusion, a *warranty* technically applies to any physical product like a tire, spoke, or valve; a *guarantee* refers to the product plus the service required to exchange the part, which fall under our service umbrella.)

By offering a warranty program, our customers could trust that when they bought a bicycle or anything else from Zane's, not only were the parts always under warranty but they were guaranteed to receive free service on replacing that part for the life of their bike. That meant that a customer could return a six-year-old bike pump for a brand-new one. Or, a customer could come in to replace her front shocks, knowing there would be no charge for the labor needed to replace them. To drive home the point behind our value package for our current and potential customers, we have *Guaranteed for Life* signs posted everywhere around the store.

Now, servicing our existing customers has become extremely easy—all that any Zane's employee ever has to say to a customer is: "You bet we will fix or replace that." Before we started this program, my employees would always be sensitive to customers trying to take advantage of us in some way, either by trying to return something that was clearly not defective or by trying to get us to throw in something extra to close a sale. Now, the conversation is simple: everything is *guaranteed* once you buy it. If you don't like it, just return it or exchange it for something you like better. Can there be a better value package than that?

After we introduced this program, our competitors who were still in business went absolutely nuts all over again. I received numerous phone calls from my competition that always started with something like, "How the heck can you do this to us?" Of course, this only made me smile. With data on our side, I knew exactly what we were doing. To begin with, we only carry quality parts from about nine vendors with whom we have built deep relationships. If I ask a vendor to make good on a returned item, I know he will because he knows I am out there selling his reputation for quality products along with my own (and if he doesn't, I'll find another vendor who will make good on it).

When you think about all the money companies spend to advertise their products in magazines and online, we're offering a bargain: it costs a vendor practically nothing to become part of our value proposition. This is how we convinced Trek to include their carbon-fiber frames in our warranty program. Even though these expensive and high-tech frames aren't designed to last as long as, say, a comparable steel or aluminum one, Trek makes good on our guarantee to replace any part on that bike because we sell more Trek bikes than anyone in the world. The number of actual returns is so small—and the potential gains so enormous— that we can quickly convince all of the vendors we work with to jump on our bus because they see where we're headed. If we are going to stand behind the service we offer our customers, we expect our supplier to do the same with their products.

Of course, some vendors needed a bit more education before they bought into our lifetime parts warranty. In the tradition of using storytelling to make my point, I often tell my employees about the helmet one of our customers brought into the store. He had lost the buckle on the helmet and had come in asking if he could buy a replacement buckle. We told him that we don't actually carry individual buckles. So, we did him one better by grabbing a brand-new helmet off the rack and handing it over to him. At first, our customer seemed hesitant to take it. But after we reminded him that everything we sell has a lifetime guarantee, his face lit up and he walked out of the store feeling better than ever about doing business with Zane's.

At the same time, I threw the old helmet in our warranty bin in our back room. Every month, we filled that bin with the parts we would be asking our vendors for credits on, which mostly involved stuff with defects. When the day came that our helmet vendor stopped in for a visit, he pulled out that helmet missing the buckle and walked up to me. "Hey, Chris, this isn't a defect, this is just missing a buckle," he said. "I realize that," I replied. "But I'd still like a credit for it."

He looked at me kind of strange for a minute before saying, "Why should I give you a credit for an entire helmet when all it has is a broken buckle?" "Simple," I said. "Because I was about to place a $5,000 order with you. And now, I'm going to call up your competitor and place it with him." Again, this guy kind of looked me over before smiling and saying, "Okay, no problem. I'll give you the credit." All I had to do was remind my vendor about the simple economics at stake. When I'm dealing with a Zane's customer, each of whom can be worth $12,500, I'm not afraid to eat the charge of a new helmet, something that might cost me $25. The same principle applies to my vendors like our helmet supplier: was he really going to jeopardize a relationship with me, one that is worth tens of thousands of dollars every year, over a single helmet? Of course not. Just as I am willing to bend over backward for my customers, I also expect my vendors to do the same for me.

And, if you'll permit me another sidebar on language, it's important for Zane's to distinguish between the terms *customer* and *partner*. I will often hear vendors referring to us as their partners, which is simply wrong—they are our *supplier*.

It's not as if they are helping us meet our payroll and pay our electricity bill; they are selling us a product that we in turn offer to our customers. We are their *customer*, and I will hold them just as accountable as our customers—from both our retail and special markets—hold us. It's not as if customers of ours who buy $1,000 bikes now consider us their partners. If those customers feel we have wronged them in any way, they have the right to take their business somewhere else. We apply that same principle to both our suppliers and our corporate customers, many of whom also fall into the trap of calling us their partner. As soon as we start thinking that these customers are actually partners, we'll get lazy. Worse, we might leave the door open to one of our competitors, who might claim that he or she can be a better partner in providing bikes to special markets. We can't allow that to happen.

At Zane's, we aren't afraid to work hard to maintain our relationships with our customers, and we expect them to make demands that please them. At the same time, we are constantly working to remind our customers how hard we are working for them, so that when one of my competitors walks through the door of one of my corporate customers and starts dropping the word *partner*, the hair stands up on the neck of that customer because he starts to smell a hard sell on its way. And that's all I ask—that my customers demand the same kind of hard work from everyone else that we continue to deliver to them every day.

• building our three-legged stool •

The third leg of our value proposition that goes along with our service and parts guarantees is our ninety-day price protection guarantee. This is just like the programs offered by the big-box retailers like Best Buy that give customers the ability to shop around and ensure that they get the lowest price on whatever they're looking to buy or have already purchased. People used to tell us, "You must be more expensive if you can guarantee everything for life."

After hearing that same phrase repeated over and over again, we eventually came to realize that our entire proposition sounded too good to be true. Human nature tells us that even though we were presenting these customers with the best opportunity around, these folks were still skeptical. We came to visualize this model as a three-legged stool built upon great products, great service, and a great price. We found that we were constantly tipping over because our customers didn't believe in the strength of our pricing leg.

That was the first reason we started the price protection guarantee because, as always, we wanted our customers to trust that we weren't trying to gouge them or give them a hard sell. But we also wanted to take the whole question of price right out of the customer's buying decision. The scenario we were trying to eliminate was when I or one of my salespeople would spend time going over the details of a particular bike, only to have the customer say at the end, "Okay, thanks for your time, I'm going to shop around a bit and get back to you." They felt like they needed to go shop around, if only to convince themselves that we weren't trying to rip them off. But that meant, of course, that these potential customers might fall prey to one of my competitors. That's why I needed to find a way to make those potential customers comfortable enough to close those sales but also to do everything in my power to keep that customer from going into one of my competitors' stores.

When we finally hit upon the ninety-day price protection guarantee, we could change the conversation. Once we were willing to guarantee that the customer could come back anytime in the ninety days after they bought a bike if they found a lower price, our customers didn't have to worry that we were somehow trying to deceive them. This also made the job of selling all that much easier for my team; now our people working the sales floor could heavily promote our lifetime service and parts guarantees, along with the promise that the customer would also be getting the lowest possible price for the bike. Once we framed the discussion this way, we took away any reason for customers to shop around because there was absolutely no reason for them to go anywhere else.

To be blunt, and to use Joe Karbo's words, not mine, "Most customers are lazy." And what I mean by that is that once we finish our pitch about the total value proposition of what we're offering, most of our customers will never go out and hunt for prices. First of all, bike shops don't advertise in those free flyers you find in your Sunday newspaper. If you were looking for a new television, sure, you could compare prices on the same model across a dozen stores in no time. But to do the same with bikes, you'd actually have to call up every name in the phone book or get in your car and visit them to do your comparison-shopping. Not many customers will go to that extreme. But, if they do, we want to make sure that they come back into our store to take advantage of their hard work.

For example, let's say a customer who just bought a bike from us for $500 happens to stop by a competitor's store and sees the that same bike for $450. Simple—we just pull the $50 difference in cash, plus 10 percent, ($5 in this case) right out of the register. And we have no interest in cluttering up the process with a bunch of paperwork either: our customer doesn't have to fill out any forms or even hand over a credit card. We like simple, so we just give him or her the $55 right then and there. Not only does this make the customer happy—"Boy, that was easy"—he or she now has $55 in hand and is standing in a place with some pretty cool stuff. And, by the way, my salesperson can conveniently point out all the great items available that will make our customer's cycling experience even more enjoyable. Again, when we focus on delivering as much value as we can to the customer, we aren't digging a hole for ourselves: we are creating scenarios where everybody wins (well, except for my competitors, of course).

Interestingly, we have never had a customer request price protection twice. You would think that if it were that easy to collect the price protection refund, every future purchase would be tested. We've found that by delivering on our promise and building an unquestionable trusting relationship in our customers' minds, we become the only bike shop that they ever visit.

• the accidental home run •

The newest leg of our value proposition, a fourth leg to add extra stability, is our flat tire insurance program—which is basically an insurance program where customers can hedge their costs of having their flat tires repaired. Tire punctures are the only things not covered by our service and parts guarantees because they are not a defect. But, truth be told, my primary motivation for starting the program was to keep my customers out of my competitors' shops. I would never have guessed that this program, which is only a few years old, would not only become one of our most requested features but that it has also become one of the most profitable aspects of our business as well.

On a case-by-case basis, changing a flat tire is probably the most profitable thing any bike shop does. Most shops charge fifteen dollars for something that costs about two dollars in parts (the tube) and takes five minutes to do (replacing the tube and then inflating it). The problem is that because every shop, including Zane's, charged about the same fifteen dollars to fix the flat, our customers could just as easily walk into the nearest competitor's store to get service. I absolutely hated this and was desperate to find a way to change the game somehow. Just like with the ninety-day price guarantee, I wanted to find a way to keep my customers from frequenting my competitors' shops. Call me a bit uptight, but I don't want to give the competition even a single chance to win one of my customers away. Plus, we became even more exposed to our customers hunting down lower prices offered whenever they walked into the door of a competitor's shop to get a flat fixed. I was willing to spend more than a few quarters to prevent those visits from ever happening.

The truth is that we have worked diligently to design the layout of our retail store to encourage our customers to browse through the latest and greatest products we have received from our vendors. In fact, even when a customer drops off a bike for a service call, he or she needs to travel from the front doors back to the repair shop—passing through what we have come to call *the gauntlet,* a corridor lined with our best merchandise, everything from flashy jerseys to handlebar-mounted trip computers. That means that every customer who drops off or picks up a bike needs to pass through the gauntlet a minimum of two times to complete his or her repair. During these trips, they will either pick up something extra or we will at least plant some seeds for something they might like to pick up on their next visit.

Grocery stores use this same principle when they place the milk in the most remote corner of their layout. To learn more about the theory behind the design of retail environments like Walmart, I highly recommend the book *Why We Buy: The Science of Buying* by Paco Underhill. (Although it will take an investment on your part to get through the entire text, it will be well worth the effort. Of course, start that one only after finishing *this* book.) The goal, of course, is to get you to buy more than the single item you originally showed up to purchase, anything from fruit rollups to those packs of candy and gum staring at you when you're trying to check out. Sure, we could allow customers to drop their bikes off at the back door, which opens into the repair shop; that would have the benefit of keeping the floors cleaner, but it would also remove all those extra opportunities to plant the seeds for present and future buying opportunities. Given how much thought and emphasis we put into this aspect of our business, you can imagine how horrible we thought it would be if our customers actually had some reason to go to a *competitor's store*, where they could fall into that retailer's trap, simply because they needed a flat tire fixed.

After spending many sleepless nights thinking through this dilemma, we finally hit upon a solution: why not create a new program where we would agree to fix an unlimited number of flat tires for a onetime fee? The customer will have made an upfront investment, so he or she will therefore have the incentive to bring his or her bike back to our shop rather than going around the corner to visit my competitor. We experimented a bit, trying to come up with the right price for the program and, in the end, $19.99 just felt right. All a customer had to do was get two flats repaired and they would come out ahead. But the lucky customers who enroll in our program get a whole lot more than just new tubes for their $19.99.

When a member of the program brings a flat into the store, the entire staff springs into action and gives him or her the red carpet treatment. We put a sticker on the rim of the tire to show that it is covered by the insurance, so we can immediately recognize that we will be treating this person as someone special. After all, we want them to feel good about trekking all the way out to our store. That means that we will not only change the flat, we'll treat that customer like gold.

We start by escorting him or her over to the coffee bar, where we pour a beverage of his or her choice. Then, our mechanics get to work fixing the flat, as well as buffing, polishing, and tuning up the bike before rolling it back out to the customer's car. Before it gets to the parking lot, though, that bike rolls right through the middle of the store where every other customer gets to gape at all the extra attention we lavish on each and every member of the flat tire club. Do you think every other customer in the store doesn't start asking about enrolling in the same program? You bet, which is why the program has become a runaway success for us— we sell about four thousand of these plans every year. But even I underestimated its true impact on the bottom line of our business.

As I mentioned earlier, I originally envisioned the program simply as a way to keep my customers away from the competition. I was fully prepared to eat the cost of all those extra tire repairs. But, after the first year, we looked at the numbers and they were eye-opening. Although I was expecting to repair hundreds of free flats each and every year, the data shows that we were only being asked to fix about fifty flats a year. What we learned is that our customers who do the most riding actually don't buy the insurance. Given that they're the ones out riding on remote backcountry roads or deep in the woods, they know how to change their own flats—otherwise they'd be doing a lot of walking. The people that buy the insurance, on the other hand, are casual weekend riders or parents buying it for their kids. You can bet that these are the same folks who buy AAA memberships so that they don't have to change a flat on their cars either.

But the success of the program truly has been in educating our customers about how to avoid getting flats in the first place, which is to keep up the air pressure in your tires; hard tires don't get flats. If we coach our customers well about this fact, we cut down on the number of repairs we have to do. It also means that the program becomes increasingly profitable. When you have four thousand new customers enrolling in the program each year paying $19.99, and only fifty of those come back each year, that means that every flat that rolls into the store is worth about $1,600 (4,000 × $19.99 / 50). When you look at the math that way, that customer who brings their flat tire in really is worth his or her weight in gold. Is it any wonder why they get the royal treatment?

Our quest for offering our customers value, however, has not always been a smooth road. The key point is that we need to keep pushing the envelope on adopting new ideas but also be willing to pull the plug on any program that isn't adding to the customer's total value proposition (or one that even begins to drain our bowl of quarters more than we'd like). This is what happened to the home-delivery program we offered a few years back. The idea was that if a customers were too busy to drop off or pick up their bikes for servicing, we would transport it for him or her. We purchased a cool-looking van with *Zane's* painted all over it and, at first, it seemed like a great idea. Heck, if even McDonalds can deliver to its New York City customers, shouldn't we be able to do the same in Branford?

Unfortunately, it didn't take long to realize that the program wasn't going to last. The biggest obstacle was trying to nail down customers about when they were going to be home. Either we wouldn't know when to show up to pick up the bike or, more commonly, no one was home when we showed up to drop a bike off. That meant that we couldn't leave the bike unattended—the last thing we wanted was for a customer's bike to be stolen after we left. The longer we continued the program, the more frustrated we got. Not only was it inconvenient for us, we were wasting plenty of money on gas and labor driving around trying to pin down our wayward customers.

We eventually pulled the plug, primarily because, unlike our service guarantee or flat insurance, it didn't seem like it was adding much value to the customers' experience. The delivery option just wasn't a swing factor for them. To add insult to injury, we were effectively keeping our customers from visiting our stores, which was limiting our chances to further our relationship with them and sell them some cool stuff. Of course, we still make good on the promises we made to those customers who bought a bike while we were running the pick-up/drop-off program. But the key point is that when stretching to include these value-added programs for your customers, nothing is permanent. When you look at these things objectively, you begin to understand that a few short-term losses are well worth the investment if your victories have shifted the rules of the game.

• changing the game •

In the end, the goal of our free service and guarantee programs is to change the naturally combative relationship that exists between buyers and sellers. Sure, we still have customers that come into our shops thinking they have figured out some new angle they're going to beat us on. But we think a lot about how the game is played and that's why we're trying to change the rules so that everyone (except my competitors) wins. If everything we have is guaranteed for life, life becomes even easier for my employees because they don't have to worry about what the customer is asking for—all a Zane's employee has to do is concentrate on building up our future relationship with the customer right in front of him or her. Meanwhile, as we'll discuss in the next chapter, we're also working to find new and creative ways to build our future customer base.

· 4 ·

planting seeds

WHEN I THINK back to my childhood growing up in East Haven, Connecticut, a town not far from Branford, where Zane's is located today, I'll never forget Phil's Canteen—one of those mobile trucks that sold food at construction sites. It wasn't that I especially liked the food or drink they had at Phil's. After all, I was nine. The reason I'll never forget that name is that Phil's sponsored my Little League baseball team. That meant I had that name, in sporty cursive, sprawled across my chest for an entire summer.

Anyone who has ever played Little League understands; the team name you play under is something you never forget. (I also remember that our team consistently put a beating on Foxon Auto Body, but the Harco Laboratories team always trounced us.) I still have no idea about what Harco Labs does or sells, even though they are located next to our headquarters, and I just never had the occasion to get my car fixed up by the guys at Foxon Auto Body. But, if I did have a chance to do business with either of them today, I know I would automatically be biased in their favor because of the connections I made with their brands way back when I was a kid. More important, as an adult, I look back in appreciation for what Phil's did to make it possible for me to play some baseball. Sure, it was a bit of advertising for them, but they were also making stronger ties to their community in the process.

I guess you could say that by getting involved in sponsoring Little League, Phil's Canteen, Foxon Auto Body, Harco Labs, and others planted the seeds of their brands with a whole generation of local schoolkids. That's why we at Zane's, on the model of Phil's, have married the notion of doing good business with doing good deeds outside the walls of the business as a way to build our own lifetime relationship with our community.

• building community ties •

Long before my three boys—Ian, Charlie, and Oliver— started playing for organized teams, Zane's was already sponsoring a Little League team. But we don't limit our efforts to baseball. We actually sponsor the entire basketball league in the town of Guilford—400 boys and 400 girls, 800 kids in all. It's a blast to see kids playing with the Zane's name scrawled across their jerseys (though, whenever possible, we keep our kids from playing on a Zane's sponsored team).

The truth is, we could never achieve the same kind of goodwill through advertising in the local media that we get for what amounts to about $2.50 for each jersey. You know what I'm talking about—you pick up your Sunday paper to see pictures of all those young faces wearing jerseys with the Zane's name on it. More recently, we have begun sponsoring local triathlons—a sport aimed at adults. We now sponsor three throughout the year, all of which are great opportunities to support local athletes competing in a challenging event that also happens to celebrate cycling. And that notion really gets to the core of what I want to bring to the community. Sure, I want to be the store my neighbors turn to when they want to purchase their next bike. But it's just as important to me to champion the sport of cycling as a whole. The way I look at it, if everyone begins riding more often, either because of our efforts or because they want to emulate Lance Armstrong's comeback at the Tour de France, Zane's as an organization can't help but benefit as a result.

When cycling gets headlines, we have to be ready to take advantage. One of my favorite stories related to this happened a few years ago when the state of Connecticut passed a mandatory helmet law for every child under the age of sixteen. There was more than a bit of controversy surrounding this law because it meant that parents would be forced to shell out a lot of extra money to buy helmets before their kids could hit the streets on their bikes. If the situation was bad in Branford, which is a relatively well-off town, it was going to be worse in the low-income, inner-city areas around the state. My competitors, not surprisingly, saw the whole scenario as a potential boon for their businesses. Kids' helmets typically wholesale at about twenty dollars and then sell at retail for forty dollars—resulting in a healthy twenty-dollar profit on each sale that gets rung up. With the expectation that potentially thousands of kids and parents would be heading their way, my competitors got busy overstocking their shelves with helmets in every size and shape in anticipation of this great windfall. I decided to use a different tactic.

Of course, I would love to cash in by selling a bunch of helmets, just like the next guy. But rather than take the usual path, I saw a much larger opportunity unfolding by changing how the game would be played, as well as a golden opportunity to plant the seeds of the Zane's brand in thousands of new lifetime customers. My first move was to call up the superintendents of each of the school districts in our area and lay out my plan. My proposal was this: I would sell helmets directly to the kids in their schools at the same wholesale price I paid to get them. That meant parents could save at least twenty dollars in getting their kids out riding again.

"What's the catch?" the superintendents would ask. "None," I would say in reply. "All I ask is for your help in administering the paperwork to pull it all off." "Easy enough," they would say. "Just contact the local PTA groups and we'll support you 100 percent."

And so I was off, placing another round of calls to the PTA groups to outline the plan. I would provide forms that the kids would fill out with their names and the circumference of their head to better determine their helmet size. The PTA would then help distribute those forms throughout the classrooms, make sure the kids brought the forms home to their parents, and then help collect the money or credit card numbers the parents sent back to school the next day. The PTA organizations even went so far as to subsidize the program to make sure that even kids from low-income families could sign up to get the same custom-fit helmets as their wealthier classmates. The last step, then, was for Zane's employees to drop off the helmets with each kid's name clearly printed on the box to each of the schools.

It was a beautifully executed plan and the local media absolutely ate the entire thing up. I still remember watching several Zane's employees on the local TV news stations as they dropped off boxes to hundreds of smiling and cheering kids. "Zane's helps kids get back on the road" was basically the gist of the news stories. The widespread coverage then sparked more interest in what we were doing back at the retail store. As soon as other school districts around the state heard what we were up to, they wanted in as well. The end result was that in just five weeks, we delivered more than 5,000 helmets (all with a Zane's sticker on the back of them) and got a ton of good press in the bargain. Not only did we do a good deed, but we used the opportunity to cement the Zane's name with a generation of kids.

Although we didn't directly pocket any profit by doing this, we did benefit the business indirectly in another way: my competitors were left with shelves stocked with all the helmets they had ordered, which prevented them, at the very least, from stocking up on new inventory. You can bet that more than a few of my competitors spent more than a few hours shouting more than a few curses in my direction as they continued to be weighed down by those boxes of unsold helmets lining their walls. In the end, the whole thing played out as one of those rare win-win scenarios that pushed us further ahead of our competition. Please take a second to recall how close this now incredibly successful helmet salesman was to losing us as a customer in the previous chapter; a $20 questionable warranty credit then for a $100,000 order—now that's a return on investment.

Just a few years after we introduced the helmet program, we found ourselves facing a similarly juicy opportunity to sow the seeds of the Zane's brand in a new set of customers. I learned that one of our competitors, a shop that is based right near the Yale University campus in downtown New Haven, always stocked up his inventory levels for the start of the school year in the fall. Even kids who already had bikes would swing by his shop to pick up accessories like bike chains and locks that they may have forgotten to pack at home. When you walked into this guy's shop each fall, his shelves would be overflowing with all this inventory: it was almost like he was already counting his profits just by looking at it. Unfortunately for him, this got me to thinking about how to change the rules on him. "Hey, these students are new members of our community, too," I thought. "Matter of fact, many of them might end up spending more than just the next four years in the New Haven area. Let's do something that they can remember us by."

With that bit of inspiration, we sprang into action. I had a couple of Zane's employees load up our delivery truck with about 1,000 bike locks custom-imprinted with the Zane's logo. I told my guys to head over to where all the student housing was near campus. Once you get there, I told them, start handing those locks out. And hand them out they did—all 1,000 in less than five hours. The kids went nuts for us and really responded well to the giveaway. The end result was that we now had 1,000 really smart kids riding around with our locks on their bikes, talking about how great Zane's was. (Meanwhile, as more than just a side benefit, my competitor was stuck with 1,000 locks gathering dust on his shelves.)

Although we still show up on campus to run a similar giveaway from time to time, it's amazing how many new customers have walked in the door of our retail shop in Branford, which is about a fifteen-minute drive from New Haven, who tell us about how great it was that time they got a free lock from us. Step one toward building 1,000 new lifetime customer relationships—complete.

• investing in the community •

Just as our helmet program and bike lock giveaway were huge successes for us, we have also received a lot of attention for the impact that our not-for-profit organization, The Zane Foundation, and our other charitable contributions have had within our community. We see the foundation as a way to give back to our neighbors, to invest in the kinds of building blocks that will make our community stronger tomorrow than it is today. We're investing in the future leaders of our community by creating a college scholarship program for seniors graduating from Branford High School.

But Zane's doesn't stop there. Although The Zane Foundation is dedicated to creating opportunities for our community's kids to go to college, we also make donations or sponsor charity events that aren't funding a thinly disguised supplement to our marketing efforts but are truly aimed at cementing the Zane's brand as a trusted member of the community. That's why we continue to sell bikes and our service at cost to just about any charity that requests something from use—requests that add up to about 200 contributions from us every year. Zane's the corporation, independent of the foundation, donates at least ten brand-new bicycles a month to local private schools and charities like the Leukemia Foundation. By donating $3,000 worth of bicycles to a good cause, we hope to show the members of our community that they can trust that we do care about them and the sport of cycling.

But we don't stop there either. We also are active in sponsoring everything from the Boy Scouts to regional bike races and triathlons to ensure those organizations and events keep our residents on the path of an active lifestyle. And, as we start to roll out Zane's locations throughout the country, The Zane Foundation, in combination with our other community-building outreach and charitable-giving programs, will continue to invest and spur new lifetime community relationships.

But, back to The Zane Foundation for a moment—it was something we started with the idea that, by investing in the educational foundation of the kids from our community, we would be making that foundation stronger by encouraging competition for our scholarship money. We started the organization back in 1989 as a registered nonprofit 501(c)3 organization. We originally started out donating the proceeds from stocking gumball-style candy machines, the kind where you slide in a quarter, twist a knob, and a bunch of candy slides down a chute and into your hand. We used peanut M&Ms because everyone loves them and they don't melt in your hand. It cost about fifteen dollars a month to stock each of the thirty candy machines we had with a Zane Foundation sticker on them. We would then collect about thirty dollars in quarters at the end of every month, which meant that we were earning about fifteen dollars a month on each of the machines for the foundation.

Unlike some other not-for-profit organizations that only ask for a one-dollar donation each month for the use of their name on similar candy machines, I made the decision early on to donate 100 percent of whatever profit was collected toward the foundation, which represented the money we put toward the scholarships we handed out to the graduating seniors at the end of the school year.

Although I once had dreams of expanding our number of collection points, we quickly ran into a problem of manpower. The problem was that I had to dedicate a day of a Zane's employee's time each month to collect the money and roll the quarters so we could deposit them in the bank. After operating in the same way for about five years, I began adding up the pros and cons of what we were doing. I figured we had two choices: either we needed to scale up the operation to five thousand machines and dedicate two full-time employees to operate them or, on the other hand, I could just start making direct contributions to the foundation from the company's profits. I chose the latter because, although my enthusiasm for tackling new ventures can often get the better of me, I had to remember that Zane's is in the business of selling experiences—not candy. Fortunately for Zane's, coming to that realization opened the door to a whole new universe of opportunities.

Today, rather than stocking candy machines, The Zane Foundation has taken on a life of its own. As a whole, the foundation has given back almost $100,000 to the Branford community. We now make an annual $5,000 contribution to the foundation that goes toward funding individual $1,000 scholarships for the top five graduates of Branford High School. Each of these five students receives a check for $1,000 that they can use toward whatever they want: college tuition, a car, or even a bike if they need one.

> We're giving this money away for academic achievement because I believe it creates a sense of competition among kids to strive to get better grades or improve SAT scores— which means that the community as a whole benefits.

We're giving this money away for academic achievement because I believe it creates a sense of competition among kids to strive to get better grades or improve SAT scores— which means that the community as a whole benefits. Kids who want that scholarship are going to put more hours into studying, which means the schools will begin seeing better overall performance in national tests like the ACT or SAT. That, in turn, means the community will experience bumps in its academic reputation and property values with it.

When I think about how everything is connected, I truly feel a sense of pride in making a contribution to our community when I get to stand up each year at the awards ceremony in front of 300 students and their families. Each year, in fact, I receive several letters from family members in attendance who thank us for what we did for their son, daughter, niece, nephew, grandson, or granddaughter. We have not only reaped an enormous amount of goodwill within the community for the scholarship program, but we have earned the trust of our neighbors. Every August, we see a sizable bump in the number of sales made to kids headed to college. In fact, August has become our second-largest sales month of the year. Many of them come to shop at Zane's, they tell us, simply because one of their friends won a scholarship and they really thought highly of us for making that happen. Now that they needed a bike for themselves, they figured that they might as well buy it from us because of the good thing we had done for their friend. And that, in the end, is all we can ask. No matter what city we're talking about, we want our customers to walk into the doors of our stores—either tomorrow or five years from now—because they know and trust us. Those are truly the seeds to starting a lifetime relationship.

• fertilizing our relationships •

When we look outside the walls of our stores for ways to cement our reputation within the community, we spend a great deal of time thinking about how we can do the same once someone honors us by visiting one of our stores. That is why our focus remains on treating our customers well when we have the chance, even though we might not reap the benefits of earning that customer's trust until days, months, or even years later on their next visit.

Take, for instance, the lifetime trade-in program Tom started for our kid customers discussed back in chapter two. The key benefit of this program is that it creates an opportunity to create a lifetime relationship, not only with the parents but with the kids who receive the bikes. The more positive thoughts those kids have about Zane's as they grow up, the better chance we have of counting them as lifetime customers. That's why we have always encouraged our customers who are parents, or are planning to be parents, to bring their kids along to the shop. We now have a kids' corner of sorts where we keep a bunch of toys, books, and a TV where kids can hang out while their parents shop around. The ironic thing is that we used to have a whole lot more entertainment available to our future customers, but we had to scale all this back. I have to admit, we have been *too successful* at times in our efforts to plant some seeds in the minds of our future customers.

Several years ago, we used to have a giant sandbox filled with Tonka trucks and toys inside the shop in Branford. This was in the era before play areas became common in fast-food restaurants like McDonalds and other kid-focused establishments. Other than a few public parks, there just weren't any good recreational areas available to kids back then. That got me to thinking that if we had a sandbox, we could offer yet another reason for parents to come visit the shop because they could entertain their children at the same time. The kids loved it.

In fact, they loved it too much. We started hearing from parents that they would be driving by the store when cries of *Waaahh!* would come from the backseat if the kids figured out that mom or dad was headed to the grocery store and not the bike shop. I remember one customer who was cajoling me because her kids wouldn't let her come anywhere near the shop without going into fits if they couldn't visit the sandbox. She was driving miles out of her way each day to avoid us. Although I have to admit I kind of enjoyed the extra attention we were getting, I eventually got the picture and we removed the sandbox and replaced it with the TV. The funny thing is that I'll bet those kids who visited us during those years we had that sandbox will remember the Zane's name when they get old enough to make their own decisions about where they want to buy a bike.

• broadening our horizons •

Although we continue to think of ways to win new customers by making positive contributions to the communities that we operate in, we are also always looking for creative ways to get the Zane's name in front of whole new sets of customers. Although most bike shops cater to their local communities, Zane's is one of the few that actually has a national presence because we had the foresight to expand into the realm of corporate rewards programs, which have helped fuel our expansion. In the next chapter, I'll talk about how we at Zane's have embraced the notion of using creative new ideas to keep pushing the limits of who we can share our unique model of customer service with. It turns out there is an endless supply of potential lifetime customers, if you have the courage to go after them.

· 5 ·

stretch your comfort zone

ALTHOUGH EVERY BUSINESS needs to keep growing to keep from starving, new opportunities can often be double-edged swords. On one hand, tackling new challenges is key to keeping a company and its employees fresh and invigorated. On the other, as I found with my Zane's Outdoor experience, not all new opportunities are created equal. That said, although I regret all that I lost over those ten weeks that Zane's Outdoor was in operation, I probably learned more over that period of time about running a business than in any four-year college program I could have enrolled in.

One of the key lessons I took away from that experience was that businesses have to be willing to recognize and then pounce on new opportunities when they announce themselves—especially if they give your business the chance to stretch its comfort zone a bit. The best example of where we successfully stretched our comfort zone was back in 1992 when, almost by accident, we launched the Special Markets division of Zane's—a segment of our business that involves us providing bikes to rewards programs run by dozens of major corporations. Donna Fenn did an excellent job of summarizing our move into this new market in an article that appeared in the November 2000 issue of *Inc.* magazine (she also touched on this part of our business in her book, *Alpha Dogs*).

Now, more than a decade after that article appeared, we have continued to grow and stretch this key segment of our business in ways I would never have imagined at the outset. The key to our success, as always, was to remember the lesson of Zane's Outdoor and keep our focus on delivering a unique experience to our customers—both the folks who received our bikes (whom we call recipients) and our corporate customers that run the rewards programs.

• opportunity knocks •

I used to have an ongoing discussion with Craig Seeger, my Trek sales rep, about how easy his job was compared to mine. All Craig had to do was make one sales call and he could unload 100 bikes to me in one fell swoop, whereas I had to apply the real hustle to find 100 other people to whom to sell those bikes. As is my custom, I spent quite a bit of time thinking about how to change that dynamic, but it wasn't until my then-girlfriend (now wife) Kathleen presented the perfect opportunity that I finally understood how I could change the rules of the game yet again. At the time, Kathleen was working in the marketing department of Chesebrough-Ponds, the consumer products company, which was then located down the road from us in Greenwich. One night, Kathleen told me about how Jay, her boss, was thinking of using bikes as a sale incentive for the launch of a new Brut product. Jay had asked Kathleen about possibly offering Trek bikes, which would be supplied from my shop. "Interesting," I thought. "This could be the chance to try something new I've been looking for."

I knew that most of my competitors steered clear of these kinds of rewards programs, which are called premiums or special markets. These programs were unappealing to most retailers because supplying bikes to these programs required them to ship complete bikes, not just unassembled versions with all their parts still in the box. Most bike dealers just weren't set up to handle the extra step of shipping and servicing these bikes. But I knew that my shop could in fact do that, if I could find the kinds of numbers that would make it worth our while to tackle it. But before I could even commit to working with Jay on a trial basis, I had to clear the whole thing with Trek. Trek only sells its bikes through dealerships like mine, and they forbid anyone from selling bikes directly to consumers over the Internet or through mail order because those sales might bite into other dealers' territories.

Determined to open some fresh ground, I set up a meeting with John Burke, who was then Trek's vice president of sales (John, who is the son of Trek's founder, Richard Burke, has since become the company's CEO). John and I go way back, but I still had to sell him on the whole idea of including Trek bikes in a corporate rewards program. He finally agreed to give me the go-ahead but with two conditions: one, we had to ship each bike directly to the recipient's home address and not to a corporate address to make sure that the bikes wouldn't be resold or diverted, and two, we would be responsible for taking any customer service calls that might result from any problems with the parts or assembly of the bikes that we did ship. John cautioned me that, with these stipulations, it would mean that we would be putting the Zane's reputation on the line with each and every bike we shipped, just as if we were selling those bikes directly out of our retail shop. After John told me this, I couldn't help but smile. "John," I said. "I wouldn't have it any other way."

• taking the premiums plunge •

Even with the go-ahead from Trek to attempt our expansion into the premiums market, we still had to make a few changes internally to make sure that we could fulfill our goal of delivering experiences and not just bikes to this new set of customers. The first challenge was to get our processes and systems up to speed to handle the first order from Che-sebrough. Jay told me that his first order would be up to 125 bikes—a massive number for us at that time because we usually had a maximum of about 450 bikes on hand in the shop at any one time. Although I was confident that my team of mechanics could handle the extra volume, I still wasn't sure I had enough bandwidth to monitor the entire order fulfillment end of the operation. Just like with our helmet program, I knew that we needed to collect specific information about the person who was to receive the bike before we could ship it to him or her. That meant we would need to send out a questionnaire that asked for each person's inseam measurement, their height, and their style of riding (meaning whether they were hard-core riders or more like weekend riders). If we were going to build bikes, we were going to do it by custom-fitting every one to each of the individual recipients. That realization led me to hire my brother Ken to oversee the entire operation, which would involve building each bike, checking it for factory defects, test riding it, and then partially dismantling it so that we could safely ship it to its final destination. And it was in this last part of the equation where I felt we could really make our mark as a brand to be remembered.

The problem that most manufacturers run into when they supply bikes to these premium programs is that the bikes require assembly before the recipient of the bike can ride it. Most manufacturers actually never even take their bikes out of the box—they just ship them as they are received off the assembly line. That means that the guy or gal who picked a bike as their reward would have to show some skill in putting the bike together or face paying their local bike shop to do it for them. Not surprisingly, most people aren't as good at putting bikes together as we are—which results in a lot of unhappy customers.

When you think you're receiving something for free, the prospect of getting in your car to go pay someone before you can even use your new free thing can be somewhat annoying. But, rather than complaining to the bike brands, these customers would be voicing their unhappiness to the company running the rewards program. In other words, the people that were paying for the bike would hear about how poorly those bikes were put together. Subsequently, the people who picked the items to include in rewards programs hated bikes. Although this prospect continued to intimidate my competitors from entering the market, I saw things differently: I smelled a huge opportunity for Zane's. This kind of program was right in our wheelhouse, and I knew we could knock it out of the park. Just like we knew that we could offer a lifetime warranty on our parts and service because we took the time to build a bike the right way, I also knew we could do everything possible to make sure that the recipients of these bikes were blown away by how easy it would be for them to get up and ride their new Trek.

If we could ship a fully assembled bike, we would, but doing that is simply impractical. So what we do instead is first fully assemble the bikes in our facility so we can test ride them. Then, after partially dismantling the bike again to fit the shipping container's dimensions, the bikes go out the door. But we haven't stopped there as we continue to improve upon our processes, with the goal of making the lives of our recipients as simple as possible after they receive one of our bikes. Under Ken's direction, we began including special tools like hex and pedal wrenches with each bike we shipped, along with a detailed instruction sheet with photographs we took in the shop to show the recipient how to put the handlebars, seat, pedals, and front wheel safely back on the bike's frame. We also attached our own toll-free number to the bike's frame so that if the recipient did run into a problem putting the bike together, he or she could immediately get one of our mechanics on the phone to sort it out as painlessly as possible.

I can admit now that at first we had no idea how many calls we might receive (and whether we had the manpower to answer all the requests). More important, I really had no clue as to whether the entire program would be a success. After all, for this to become more than just a one time shot in the dark, Chesebrough would also have to consider the program a success. In the end, my fears were unfounded: not only did Jay's incentive program help him beat his sales goal for Brut by 184 percent, but we also received only about fifteen calls on the 125 bikes we delivered. Even better, there wasn't a single complaint or dissatisfied customer among the whole bunch.

Whether I realized it at the time or not, we were now squarely in the special markets business. And what we learned through the entire experience was that when someone expects to receive something for free, they actually have extremely low expectations about what they will receive. It's almost as if they're asleep—not really actively participating in the process. As long as what they ordered or were told they would receive actually shows up, like they don't receive a blender instead of a microwave, the customer will be sufficiently happy. That meant that as part of reinventing the wheel, as we started taking measurements and e-mailing shipping updates, we could actually have a far greater impact on the customers' satisfaction level than if they had walked into our store. We could instantly wake people up with a jolt of positive energy.

After discovering how well our culture fit into these kinds of opportunities, we realized we had stumbled into a ripe new area of growth for our business. The only trouble was finding how to tap into more opportunities.

At about the time we were discovering the potential of the premiums market, Volkswagen and Trek were running a joint national ad campaign, where customers who bought a new Limited Edition Jetta Trek automobile received a new Trek bike along with it. With my confidence in the potential of these rewards programs soaring, I wanted in on this. In fact, I kept pestering Craig, John, and anyone else I could pin down at Trek to let Zane's do the supply and fulfillment for the entire Trek program. Volkswagen, though, liked the fact that the Trek dealer in whatever part of the country the car was sold would be the one to provide the bike. That meant that before we could get a crack at the big time, we first had to prove that we could handle both delivering and servicing thousands of bikes on the national scale that

Volkswagen required. That's really all I needed to hear to give me the push to kick things into high gear.

Although I didn't land the Volkswagen program at that time, I did begin uncovering other opportunities to participate in corporate rewards programs. In 1996, we signed a contract with General Mills to deliver Trek bikes to grocery stores that ordered a certain amount of cereal. We also signed up Tropicana, where we supplied bikes for its "Juicy Rewards" program. Customers could accumulate the UPC codes from orange juice containers and then trade them in for prizes, including Trek bikes. When we sketched out the potential needs of its program, Tropicana initially contracted with us for 200 bikes, figuring that's all it would need. To get a new bike, customers would need to collect and send in 1,000 UPC codes, which was a heck of a lot of OJ.

Little did Tropicana know that New York's sanitation workers would soon be combing the city's trash armed with box cutters in search of discarded cartons. I remember one garbage man actually had enough points to get fourteen bikes all by himself. The result was that we ended up shipping between 20 and 100 bikes each *week* the program ran, which eventually added up to more than 2,500 bikes in all. Although Tropicana was somewhat upset about having blown its budget, shipping and servicing that many bikes gave us a huge amount of confidence that we could now handle big national deals like the Volkswagen program.

After we nailed down a few more success stories in the following years, Trek finally agreed that we were ready to take over the Volkswagen fulfillment, despite some concerns from a few of the other Trek retailers. It seems that most of the other Trek dealers weren't all that excited about participating in the Volkswagen program anyway because they could only clear about $50 on bikes that they could sell at retail for $450. Given the amount of effort involved, they simply didn't have the interest. I, on the other hand, was ecstatic for the chance to step into the breach. Reps from both Trek and Volkswagen came out to our facility, so we got the chance to show off all of our tracking and quality control systems to prove that we were both trustworthy and capable of servicing a national program. We then delivered and serviced most of the bikes sold as part of the Trek Jetta program over the next three years—a total of about 14,000 bikes between 1996 and 1998—which added up to another huge confidence booster for the company and for me personally. Even before that Volkswagen program began winding down, though, I began to think more and more about how we could keep expanding on what we were doing in the premiums market. We had just scratched the surface of its long-term potential and I wanted to dig deeper.

• shifting into high gear •

Even before we achieved our success with the cereal and orange juice programs, I had begun attending the trade shows that targeted the whole special markets industry. I even went so far as to drag my reps from Trek to a convention in Chicago to show them how much potential this industry had. Although the total retail bicycle market in the United States is worth something like $2.5 billion, the annual market for premiums and incentives was almost ten times as large—$23 billion. Those numbers could represent amazing new growth opportunities for both Zane's and Trek. But, as I attended trade show after trade show, I found that the premiums market was difficult to crack: like anything, it was who you knew, and I just didn't know the right people. Even as I allowed myself a shred of discouragement, I had a revelation—George Kling.

I had run into George at one of the special markets trade shows I attended a few years earlier. He had recognized and come up to me—turns out that George was actually a resident of Branford and a customer of Zane's (he had bought his grandson a bike from us). After our introduction, he asked me why I was at that particular show. After telling him about my interest in entering the premiums market, he told me I should hire him.

Turns out, George was a consultant who helped national companies like AT&T, Crabtree & Evelyn, Gillette, Izod, and Lacoste tap into this lucrative premiums market. At the time, though, I thought, "Heck, I've made it this far by myself. I've heard about how much consultants cost and how they can often steer a company down the wrong track. Thanks, but no thanks." Despite my lack of interest, George was very gracious and asked me to keep in touch. Well, a few years later, as I still struggled to get my foot in the special markets door, I remembered George and thought, "What the heck do I have to lose?"

Just a few weeks after placing a call into George, he was in our offices to give a presentation to a group that included Ken and me. After listening to George for just a few minutes, I began to realize how much I didn't know or simply didn't understand about this new arena. George detailed all the different avenues through which a product could be brought into a rewards program, a list that included everyone and everything from promotional agencies to catalogs that exclusively published all things related to incentive programs.

The more George talked, the more I began to understand that there were major barriers to entry to this market—only they weren't related to money or competitive position but to terminology and relationships instead. It became increasingly obvious that I wouldn't be able to grow this business any farther without George's help. At the same time, I wasn't sure I wanted to pay the $60,000 George wanted as a retainer. After struggling and going back and forth, it was my wife, Kathleen, who reminded me that with George behind me, making the leap to the next level of the premiums market would actually be a lot less risky and less expensive than all the money I blew when I opened Zane's Outdoor, the last time I tried to branch beyond the retail bike world. With that bit of good sense ringing in my ears, I hired George, and his work immediately began to pay dividends.

Before we had George on board, we had trouble connecting with anyone in the industry because Zane's was still an unknown commodity to this market. And, in hindsight, I don't blame them. If you were the guy in charge of the American Express rewards program, would you bet your job on a company you didn't know anything about? Even if the program manager from Amex might not be overly excited about working with the guy who currently supplied the bikes to his program, at least he knew who he was and what he could expect from him. In other words, there wouldn't be any surprises. When we came knocking, Zane's represented a gamble, a step into the unknown that had far more downside than upside for those running the programs. With George at our side, however, those doors started opening. Almost miraculously, all of the phone calls we made suddenly began getting picked up by the reps from the companies we wanted to work with.

Within the first thirty days after George joined the Zane's team, we got introduced to something like sixty different people connected to the premiums market—most of whom we are still working with today. George also helped us hire sixteen independent special markets reps around the country (we now have more than twenty-four), who also went knocking on doors on Zane's behalf. It wasn't long before we had more new opportunities than we could handle. By the end of that first year, we pulled in more than $2.2 million from our premiums division and it was easy to see that if we kept pushing, we could easily double that figure the following year.

It didn't take long before we had to make a few capital investments to ensure that we could continue to deliver a steady supply of bikes to all the programs with which we had contracts. The first investment we made was to purchase a 20,000-square-foot warehouse just a mile down the road from the retail shop. Ken took the responsibility of converting that warehouse into our assembly and distribution center for our premiums products. He then hired eight new mechanics, cross-trained them on all the assembly and disassembly processes that we had been using, and then set up a rotating three-man assembly line that helped us to build and test ride up to 100 bikes each and every day. We ended up spending a total of about $200,000 fitting out the building, computer systems, and tools we needed to set up a reliable delivery system that wouldn't let us or our customers down.

Building bikes can actually be quite tedious—we jokingly equate it with the line from the old Dunkin' Donuts TV commercial: "Time to make the donuts." Assemblies can be particularly tough to keep up with, given the distractions of our retail environment, such as when we have a lot of customers walking in. That's why we eventually moved all the assembly work that we used to do at the retail shop over to the warehouse. Doing so freed up the guys working in the retail shop to focus exclusively on customer-related repairs and service. The guys in the warehouse now work in an environment where they can play their music loud and take lunch breaks without having to worry about servicing a customer walking in the door.

Having these two separate environments also gives us the chance to shift and transfer guys and gals to whichever space they are most comfortable working in. Some prefer to just focus on the bikes while others are natural salesmen. Still, the focus of both groups of employees is the same: to make sure that we keep our customers' best interests in mind by focusing on building and servicing bikes to the best of our ability.

Successfully looking out for our customers by taking care of the recipients also requires some patience and a sense of humor from time to time. A more recent example was a program we ran in the New York City area for the Discovery Channel to promote its newest channel, Green Planet. To be eligible for the giveaway—a brand-new Trek bicycle—potential winners had to fill out a lengthy questionnaire that was printed in the *New York Post*. These folks also had to complete an essay of several hundred words as well, which in total was quite a bit of work to earn the right to win one of the 300 bikes being given away.

You can imagine our surprise, then, when a few weeks later, after the bikes began arriving at the winners' homes, we started receiving phone call after phone call from recipients wondering why we were delivering them a bike. Apparently, the winners hadn't remembered entering the contest, a fact that might have been confounded because the bikes they received were branded with the bright green colors of the Green Planet brand without really mentioning the connection to the Discovery Channel.

Regardless of why they were confused, after a quick explanation from us, these folks were more than happy with their prizes. All but one that is: we got word back from UPS that one recipient had refused delivery of her bike. Concerned, we called her up to explain that she had won the bike through the Discovery Channel promotion. After a minute of silence, she thanked us for calling and said she would call us right back. Sure enough, a few minutes later, she called back to explain that when she first saw the bike, she somehow jumped to the conclusion that someone had stolen her identity. Panicked, she had not only refused delivery of the bike, but she had called up and canceled all of her credit cards as well. Now, obviously embarrassed, she told us she wanted the bike and that she would pay for us to reship it to her. But, she needed to borrow her son's credit card before she could do so. Obviously, we have had some good laughs with this story over the years. "Someone stole my identity" has become somewhat of a punch line anytime something unexpected happens within the business.

The overarching key to the success of our move into the premiums market has been, just like it has been with our retail operation, our attention to our customers. The difference is that in the retail environment, our customer is the man or woman standing in front of us; in the premiums market, our customer is someone who is staring at a spreadsheet attempting to select the best vendor for his or her company's rewards or incentive program.

We now have hundreds of these kinds of customers, many of whom might buy only ten to twenty bikes a year from us. The way we go out of our way to please our corporate customers and stand out among our competitors is to make sure that they never hear a bad word from the recipients, those folks to whom we are delivering the bikes. That means that we need to work hard at building and sizing our bikes, as well as delivering them on or ahead of schedule.

In the beginning, we actually ran into some opposition from our corporate partners about sending out questionnaires to the recipients; some companies didn't want to hand over control of those relationships to us. That's when we brought the discussion back to the low expectation levels their customers actually had about receiving their free merchandise. In fact, if one of their customers had a bad experience, it could actually diminish the value of the corporate brand. By hiring us, on the other hand, these companies would be bringing in not only a steward of their brand but someone who could actually increase the value of that brand in the minds of their customers.

 The overarching key to the success of our move into the premiums market has been, just like it has been with our retail operation, our attention to our customers. The difference is that in the retail environment, our customer is the man or woman standing in front of us; in the premiums market, our customer is someone who is staring at a spreadsheet attempting to select the best vendor for his or her company's rewards or incentive program.

One of the essential keys in building our successful track record with programs like Chesebrough, Tropicana, and Volkswagen was that we could prove to these customers that when Zane's delivered bikes to their customers, we eliminated all the unnecessary phone calls that used to come in to that company's call center. By including the tools, instructions, photos, and a toll-free number to connect to one of our mechanics, we had changed the game. Meanwhile, our few competitors never even bothered to crack the boxes on their bikes before they shipped them on to the recipient—which only helped us stand out by comparison. But, as always, we continue to strive to do even better. That's also why we spend about $80,000 a year on sets of small tools, which we include along with each and every bike we deliver. I don't have to spend that money, but I do because it goes a long way toward making the lives of the bikes' recipients easier, which makes life better for my customers. (Remember the lesson about the bowl of quarters we talked about back in chapter two.)

We also have never failed to make good on an order: we have a 100 percent fulfillment rate, something that is unheard of in the drop-ship industry. Even if we had to go and buy bikes from a competitor to ensure that we could fill an order, we would do it without delay, all with the goal of pleasing both our customer and the recipient of the bike. That's why we're now considered not only the best bike supplier to the market but one of the industry's premier drop-shippers as well.

Basically, we've built switching costs into our customer relationships. That means, over time, we have erected a few formidable barriers to entry for our competition, who now have to answer why they, too, aren't doing the things Zane's does for their rewards program recipients, such as collecting measurements and supplying those tools. As a result, we have become the current, top-of-mind supplier for our corporate customers. We now put pressure on our competitors to come up with a way to sell themselves as doing something better than we are already doing. And, as you can imagine, it's not like I'm going to let that happen without a fight.

• a natural progression •

When Donna Fenn's article came out in *Inc.* in 2000, one of the things she wrote about was how I had refused to expand our drop-ship operation beyond delivering bikes. Although I had plenty of offers to expand into shipping rewards items like inline skates or even bike accessories like helmets and pumps, I had steered clear of anything that was outside of our core strength. Given that inline skates didn't need to be removed from their boxes to be assembled or serviced in any way, I didn't see how we could add any value to our customers or the recipients.

As Donna quoted me saying back then, "You put them in a box, and you send them out. Where's the service point of difference? I wouldn't have the assurance of knowing that I'm bringing something of value to the table." And, until recently, I believed what I told Donna back then.

Today, however, things have changed. As we became better and better at the shipping and distribution component of our business, I came to realize that we did indeed have something valuable to offer our customers interested in things beyond bikes; we could efficiently move inventory like few other companies out there. We had built a better mousetrap when it came to fulfilling orders for these kinds of programs.

Our $200,000 investment in our warehouse and computer systems was now paying off in ways that I never could have anticipated. The value proposition offered to our customers had now expanded to include the benefits of working with high volume on a large scale. Because we worked with so many different partners, we could move a palate of inventory in a week. If a company wanted to stock that product for itself, it might sit on a palate for an entire year—which could be death in a highly volatile market like software or electronics where the life cycles are so short. A stack of last year's hottest holiday gaming hit that might have been worth $100,000 could quickly become valued at something like $20,000 when the new season's sequel came out to replace it. Rather than having to make a huge commitment to a particular piece of inventory or even footing the cost of managing a warehouse, one of our partners could now just ask us to supply it instead—which would eliminate most of the risk on their part with a single phone call. Almost by accident, we had found yet another way to alleviate our customers' pain in a major way.

As soon as other companies that run corporate incentive programs started recognizing Zane's as the only dropshipper worthy of a gold rating two years in a row, as well as the recipient of the "Golden Carrot," an honor bestowed upon the industry's top performers, new customers started knocking on our door, asking if we would be willing to supply everything from bike racks and baby strollers to Xbox and Nintendo Wii video gaming systems. As a matter of fact, we really proved our worth over the 2007 holiday season with the Wii—a product so hot that just about no one could keep it in stock, let alone offer it as part of an incentive program. But when Maritz came calling, asking us if we could supply the Wii for its rewards program, we found a supplier who guaranteed us a supply of about 10,000 of the gaming systems.

The only catch was that we would have to pay a premium that was considerably higher than even the retail price to secure them. Maritz agreed to pay the premium and, as a result, became the only rewards program that offered and delivered access to the Wii that holiday season to its members. Afterward, we not only received a ton of positive feedback from the folks at Maritz, but they asked us to be their exclusive supplier of bike-shop-quality bikes for future programs.

So, by stretching our comfort zone into new products and services, we have both opened new doors for our core bike business and established a bit of a hedge in case, God forbid, there is a slack in the demand for bikes (which is looking quite unlikely the way gas prices have been headed lately). As long as we continue to deliver on our promises and, even more important, continue to listen to our customers' needs, we can continue to expand. I believe that we can now deliver just about any product out there that our customers ask us to supply—which, in and of itself, has become yet another competitive advantage for us. As long as we continue to focus on listening to what our customers ask us to do and finding ways to make their lives easier and more productive, who knows where our natural progression will take us next.

· 6 ·

game-changing
tactics

I HAVE TO admit that the part of my job I enjoy best is thinking up new ways to put pressure on our competition. Whether implementing new marketing programs or just coming up with creative ways to change the rules of the game, I love annoying the heck out of my competitors. Although our rivals might think they're in the same business as Zane's, our focus on selling experiences means we actually think and act differently than they do, which gives us a formidable advantage. By the time one of my competitors thinks they have figured out how to copy what we do at Zane's—either on our retail or corporate end—we've already moved on to establish a new barrier for them to overcome.

We have been pushing the envelope from the very first days I owned my shop in terms of the kinds of services we offer our customers so that they wouldn't ever think about leaving us for the competition. Even as a sixteen-year-old when I first bought the bike shop, I recognized that the best and perhaps the only way I could differentiate myself from the seventeen other competitors in the area, and especially the "big boxes," was to offer customers services they couldn't get anywhere else. That's how the idea of a one-year free service guarantee grew into today's lifetime free service and parts guarantee that we discussed in detail in chapter two.

Today, we can attract customers from all over the country that value our services more than the next guy offering the lowest price and, perhaps more important, more than the bike shop around the corner from their homes. The same principle applies to the corporate side of our business, where we can stand on our track record of eliminating customer service calls and delivering our bikes on time while our competitors can merely offer up promises of what they *might* be able to do. By embracing the idea of selling an experience and offering superior customer service, we have not only leveled the playing field, we have actually tipped it in our favor. But my competition continues to be slow to recognize this fact. In their attempts to match our service and parts guarantees, they're actually putting their businesses further and further behind us because they're not really buying into the key principles that make those programs so successful for us.

Basically, rival shops offer up their own service guarantees only because they believe it will help them sell to the customer standing in front of them. In fact, other shops *hate* offering warranties or guarantees of any kind because they see such programs only as drains on their profits, rather than as the means to win lifetime relationships. As soon as a customer comes into their shop for a repair, they'll try to find some way to charge him or her for *something* that didn't quite make it under their warranty, say a fifteen-dollar wheel alignment, for example.

What these guys don't understand or appreciate is how much tacking on that extra charge annoys their customers. Consider the customer who thought they were comparing apples to apples when they were comparing the guarantee programs at Zane's and one of our competitors. But, as soon as that customer brings the bike back in for a tune-up, my competitor has already thought of some way to squeeze something extra out of that customer like an extra part of the service that conveniently wasn't covered by the guarantee.

By acting this way, these guys prove that they simply don't see the $12,500 forest beyond those nickel-and-dime trees standing in front of them. Not that I mind all that much, of course, because that just gives us more opportunities to convert our rival's customer into our own lifetime customer. Unlike our competitors, we focus hard on making sure that the bikes we assemble and repair never have any reason to make it back into the shop. Our goal has always been to get our customer to buy their next *bike* from us, not their next spoke or brake cable.

I'm amused when I hear that my competitors have been bad-mouthing Zane's to the customers in their shop, usually by saying something along the lines that Zane's prices are too high or that we really don't make good on our promises. When these stories come back to me, I always get a smile on my face because I know we've just won another battle. I've also received many phone calls directly from these same competitors begging me for mercy. Imagine you pick up your phone to hear the voice on the other end of the line say, "Hey, Chris, I'll drop this lifetime free service guarantee if you will. Then, we can just compete on price like every other business out there."

> Compete on price? Ha! These guys just never seem to get it. The last thing I want to do is get involved in some kind of race to the bottom; that's Walmart's territory.

Compete on price? Ha! These guys just never seem to get it. The last thing I want to do is get involved in some kind of race to the bottom; that's Walmart's territory. If we were so foolish as to go up against the biggest of the big boxes, both my competitor and I would soon find ourselves out of business. My competitors simply continue to outthink themselves, and I'm stealing their customers as a result. Although their profits are drying up, at Zane's, we continue to grow our revenues by 23 percent each and every year—a rate we expect to double, perhaps even triple, once our national expansion plan is in place. With that track record to give us the confidence to keep pushing the envelope of how creative we can be in our business, I continue to have a blast by rolling out new programs or thinking up new ways to keep our competition scrambling to keep up with us.

• drive your competitors nuts •

Coming up with new ways to annoy my competition doesn't just make for good entertainment; it makes for good business. Consider the story about the helmet program we ran for Connecticut kids that I wrote about back in chapter four. Do you think that move might have annoyed my competitors, as they watched shelves loaded with thousands of unsold helmets collecting dust while Zane's employees and our logo were flashed on all the local TV stations? We turned what should have been a profit bonanza for our rivals into warehouses full of red ink and a lot of positive advertising for us.

As another example, think back to the bike lock giveaway we orchestrated on the Yale University commons, where we basically left my biggest competitor stuck with a season's worth of bike locks because we struck first by handing out 1,000 free locks to the incoming students with a big Zane's logo on them. Do you think that guy had an unkind word or two for me over the years as those potential customers started walking in the doors of our shop instead of his?

Also consider our flat tire insurance program, which I discussed back in chapter three. The truth is that, although that program is an extremely profitable component of our retail business, I started it simply to keep my customers from walking into my competitors' shops to get their tires fixed. It bugged me to no end to think that my customers might have a reason to visit one of my competitors and, worse, spend some money in another shop simply because it happened to be closer to their homes. Today, we not only have a program that gives our customers an incentive to come back to us, it creates pressure on my competitors to come up with something similar or risk losing their existing customers to us.

Yet another example of how we applied this kind of competitive pressure involved one of my earlier promotions, in which I was one of the first companies in the country to give away cell phones. Of course, free phones are all too common today. But at one time, this was a radical practice. By tying the free phone to the purchase of any new bike, I was able to create a hugely effective advertising campaign at very little cost to our bottom line. The key was realizing that most companies that sold phones for the phone carriers and manufacturers pocketed some profit on the sale of the phone, as well as receiving a commission on each new customer activation. At that time, phone companies were paying $250 for every new customer you could sign up, although the phone cost $225. I figured that I could clear in profit an amount over and above what I would make from the sale of the bike, as well as usage commission from the phone company and a co-op advertising allowance the phone company also paid out. When I added up all the numbers, it was clear that this was a golden opportunity I couldn't pass up. I soon got myself licensed as an independent phone dealer and rented a billboard—which the phone company paid for—to promote the giveaway: "Buy a bike from Zane's and receive a free cell phone."

Within hours of the sign going up, tons of new customers poured into our shop—a steady stream that didn't let up for months. We ended up with one of our most profitable quarters in Zane's history. Meanwhile, my competitors were left with the choice of scrambling to offer a similar program of their own or be left standing still in an empty shop.

We continue to push the creative envelope with our marketing service programs today. We have embraced technology for some help in rolling out innovations like a live Internet-accessible Web-cam into our tech center, where customers can connect and watch how to make their own corrections or repairs. With Skype, which allows us to communicate via voice and video over the Internet in real time at virtually no cost, we can communicate with the corporate recipients of our bikes on how to make a necessary adjustment, regardless of where that person lives. We also use e-mail to stay in touch with both the retail and corporate customers in our database. For our rewards programs recipients, we can stay in touch after they've selected a bike from a rewards program by passing along the shipping and tracking numbers so that they aren't forced to wonder when it might be arriving.

But e-mail can be a powerful and inexpensive marketing tool as well. Although my competitors spend big money on advertising in local newspapers and on highway billboards, we can produce customized outreach programs that are both virtually free and incredibly effective. For example, because we collect our customers' heights and inseams to custom-fit their bikes, we can send out zero-cost reminders about new inventory we might have just received in their size or even a coupon they can use the next time they visit the shop. Once we have potential customers hearing about programs and promotions like these, it never takes long before those folks begin asking my competitors why they aren't offering a similar service. Of course, all my competitors think about is, "Jeez, how much is that going to cost me to set up?" rather than how they might put something similar—or even better—in place as an effort to leapfrog me. The goal, again, is to keep changing the game on our competitors so they're always trying to keep up. I never want to give them a chance to catch their breath—or focus on moving ahead of me.

• drive up the price tag on talent •

Another surefire way to get under your competitors' skin is to make it difficult for them to hold on to their best employees. As with any business, recruiting and retaining top-notch employees can be an endless headache for an owner. Not only are good people hard to find, nothing is quite so gut-wrenching as when an employee in whom you have invested thousands of dollars and years of training walks away to work for one of your competitors. That's why, on one hand, we do everything we can to make Zane's a fabulous place to work. On the other, by embracing this concept, I want to make it as hard as possible for my competitors to hang on to their best people. In other words, I have from time to time engaged in efforts to poach talent from my competitors or, failing that, to make it much harder for that guy to continue operating by making his employees more expensive to keep around. Let me explain what I mean in the context of a recent story.

As I mentioned earlier, we hear feedback from a few of our customers that one of our competitors has been bad-mouthing some aspect of how we do business at Zane's. These customers of ours are acting almost like undercover agents on our behalf because the stories they collect usually involve customers stopping in at a competitor's shop and asking if they happen to offer programs similar to our lifetime guarantees. The response that these customers relay back to us is that the guys working the sales floor at our competing shops respond to the questions by saying things like, "Listen, Zane's is full of it. They're trying to rip you off. That Chris Zane is full of hot air. They don't really offer free service; that's just a scam. We'll treat you right if you buy your bike from us."

After hearing about one too many of these competing managers trying to spread some dirt on Zane's, I decided to do something creative to end this particular smear campaign; I called up the offending store manager, let's call him Pete, and offered him a job at Zane's. I had heard that Pete was actually a pretty effective manager, so I thought if I could lure him away, I would not only cause my competitor a lot of pain, but I could acquire an effective employee as well. After I made my pitch, the first answer I got from Pete was a minute or two of silence. At first, he seemed more than a little nervous—and maybe even suspicious. After breaking the ice a bit by making a joke or two, I then asked him how much he was making. "Fifteen dollars an hour," he said.

Now it was my turn to deliver a moment of silence. "Man, your boss is underpaying you big-time," I said. "I'll give you $17.50 if you come work for me." I received more stunned silence in response: I had obviously struck a nerve. A $100-a-week raise obviously meant something to this guy. After clearing his throat, Pete thanked me for the offer but told me he needed to think about it. He said he had been working for his boss for a long time and that he owed him the chance to match the offer. "No problem," I replied. "Get back to me in a week."

After a week or so went by, Pete called me up to tell me that his boss matched my offer. "Okay," I said. "He's still underpaying you. I'll pay you $20 an hour to come work for me. We have an opening we think you'd be perfect for and we're willing to spend some money to put any new ideas you come up with into action." I received some more stunned silence in response. Pete eventually thanked me for my second offer, but, again, he needed to run it by his boss before he could say yes. "No problem," I said, "I'll call you in a week."

When I got back in touch with Pete, he gave me his final answer. "Chris, I really appreciate your offer, but my boss matched the $20 and this shop is so much closer to my house. I have to say no to you." I told him that was fine. But

I also reminded him that, thanks to me, he did just receive an $800-a-month raise. In return for that, I asked Pete for a favor: please quit the smear campaign against Zane's.

And to Pete's credit, he did just that. We stopped hearing any faulty information originating from Pete's store about all those supposed bad things we were up to. That turn of events alone was worth the time and effort involved in my attempts to hire Pete. Even if he had accepted my offer, I knew we would still make sure he was a fit with our culture and, if he wasn't, I wouldn't be afraid to let him go (plus, if we let him go within ninety days of hiring him, he would count against my competitor's unemployment insurance premium, not mine). It may seem mean-spirited and certainly not my first choice, but understanding all aspects of our business is imperative. If he worked out, though, *Wham!* I would have had another crack sales manager working for me. The best part about the whole story, though, is that I just bumped up my competitor's overhead by $800 a month—which might be a month's utility bill or possibly even another employee's salary that he would be forced to lay off to balance his budget. Either way, it was a win-win scenario for Zane's.

There is also an interesting side note to this story: I've actually tried to lure away a competitor's store manager on three different occasions, and each time I failed to persuade the manager to leave his employer to come work at Zane's. But it never mattered because each time we tried it, we changed the game just enough on our competitors to continue to make it more interesting—and more expensive— for them to keep playing.

• keep the pressure on •

I'll admit that whenever I think back to what I consider some of our more inventive and somewhat off-the-wall ideas for keeping the pressure on our competitors when they least expect it, I laugh out loud a bit.

One of the stories I often share when I speak in front of seminars or college students involves one of my competitors who ran a bike shop in Clinton, Connecticut, which is just a few miles east of our Branford location. Even though his shop was small, it was in a decent location in the middle of downtown, right next to a popular pizza joint. But when this guy's lease was up, he moved in the middle of the night to a larger location a few miles down the road.

One day as I was driving through downtown Clinton, I noticed that the shop was empty, so I pulled into the parking lot to investigate. I found out that the same folks who ran the pizza restaurant owned the building the cycle shop was in. After talking to the owners, I found out that my competitor had moved out without giving any notice, which left his former landlords high and dry and scrambling to find a new tenant.

"Listen," I told the owners. "What would you say if I paid you $200 cash a month to put a sign in the window that would say, 'Bike Shop Closed. Please visit our friends at Cycle Madison' along with our address and telephone number?" (Cycle Madison was a nearby shop of which I was a co-owner.)

The owner of the pizza joint was thrilled with the idea. "Deal," he said with a smile. Of course, my competitor should have done right by his former landlord and he could have posted his own sign redirecting his customers to his new location. He just didn't imagine that someone like me would think to take advantage of his mistake.

The end result was that for the next few months, dozens of my competitor's confused customers drove up to his former location wondering what had happened. Apparently, they hadn't realized that he had moved. Fortunately for them, our sign quickly redirected them to our sister store location to get their repairs or buy their new bike—business that should have belonged to my competitor. For what added up to about a $1,000 investment on my part, we acquired dozens of potential lifetime customers.

One of the key points of keeping pressure on your competitors by driving them nuts is to get them thinking about what you're doing, always focused on catching up rather than focusing on innovating and improving on the aspects of their own business. I'm always looking for ways to distract them and throw them off their game—outdoing their new billboard with one of my own across the street, for example, or taking out a half-page ad in the Yellow Pages that outclasses their postage-stamp-sized ad. It's like jumping into a boxing match where I'm not just trying to keep from getting hit, I'm trying to make my opponent think about what I might do next rather than focusing on what his best next move should be. Think about how well Apple has gotten into the heads of the folks at Microsoft. Think those ads that equate Apple with young, tech-savvy people and Microsoft with an over-the-hill, middle-aged guy don't have some effect on the psyche of everyone in Redmond?

One of the best examples of how well this strategy can work for Zane's involves the annual Big Wheel Sale we hold every spring. As I mentioned previously, this sale is absolutely *huge* for us; it accounts for more than 15 percent of our annual sales. And we make a big deal about it by spending big to promote it in all the regional media. Our vendors even come out for the weekend to enjoy seeing their products sell by the truckload. Of course, all the attention we receive tends to annoy the heck out of our competition.

A few years ago, a few of our competitors tried to create a big sale of their own. Two shops, one in West Haven and another in Branford, both touted their own HUGE sale in a series of expensive billboards and with TV advertising. They had me on edge for a while, wondering what they might be up to. It's too bad for my competitors that their whole strategy backfired.

When the big day arrived, some of our customers came and told us that they had stopped by our competitors' sales to see what the buzz was about and that it was a huge letdown. Whereas we literally have 1,400 bikes on display during the sale, our competition had a few dozen bikes parked out on their lawn. Not only did their attempts at creating buzz not generate enough traffic to compete with us, the lack of anything interesting going on actually created negative feelings among the potential customers who stopped in because the whole event fell so short of their expectations.

Later on, I learned from someone who worked for one of my competitors that they felt their version of the sale was a big success because they had sold twenty-five bikes over the entire weekend. "We sell twenty-five every single day of the year," I thought. If we only sold twenty-five bikes on the biggest day of the year for us, we'd probably be out of business by now as well (yep, the West Haven store went out of business). The point of this example is that, rather than trying to find a way to leapfrog us, maybe by creating a unique event involving a shoreline ride or even a carnival or something, my competition just tried to chase me at my own game (offering, in their mind, a "HUGE" sale) and, as a result, lost big.

• take advantage of defunct competitors •

One of the best ways to attract new customers to your business is to work like crazy to put your competitors out of business and then use some creativity to take advantage of some new opportunities they leave behind. One great example of this was back in the early 1990s, when we at Zane's started paying the phone company to forward the calls made to out-of-business bike shops to our own. At that time, a bunch of mom-and-pop bike shops had closed down and the total number of shops in the area dropped from fourteen to five. It seemed like every day brought a new Going Out of Business Sale.

> One of the best ways to attract new customers to your business is to work like crazy to put your competitors out of business and then use some creativity to take advantage of some new opportunities they leave behind.

As soon as one of these shops went under, I would call up the phone company and get them to forward any calls placed to that number directly to our retail hotline. (This has since become common practice and a source of a lot of extra revenue for the phone companies, by the way.) A lot of those shops still had ads running in the Yellow Pages, so if a prospective customer dialed the number, they would reach us instead. Plus, any bikes that shop had sold over the years had a sticker with the shop's phone number stuck to its frame. As the customers who bought those bikes needed service or a replacement, they would simply look at the number on their bike and ring it up. Only, instead of being connected to New Haven Bicycle and Sport or Alpha Lo Bicycles, they would hear a message that said something like, "The number you are calling is no longer in service, press 0 to be connected toll-free to Zane's Cycles for all of your cycling needs."

Not only did this bring in plenty of extra calls for Zane's, it gave these potential new customers the notion that somehow the phone company was endorsing our business, which gave us a little bit of bonus credibility before we even struck up a conversation.

We've also been able to purchase phone numbers from a defunct competitor outright so that a customer calling that number would be connected directly to our retail shop. I remember receiving such a call a few years ago from a prospective customer who was trying to gauge the price for a new bike he wanted. I happened to be working the phones that day from inside my office. I was in the middle of some paperwork when the phone rang.

"Hello, you've reached the world-famous Zane's Cycles," I said in my friendliest voice.

"How much are you guys asking for a Trek 820?" the caller asked.

"That model is selling for $269.99," I replied.

"Thanks," he replied and quickly hung up before I could get in another word.

Five minutes later, another call came in. "Hello, you've reached the world-famous Zane's Cycles," I said into the phone.

"How much are you guys asking for a Trek 820?" the caller asked. "It's selling for $269.99," I replied before I could register anything.

"Thanks," the caller said and quickly hung up.

After a minute, I thought, "That was weird. Was that the same guy?"

After another five minutes went by, the phone rang again.

"Hello, you've reached the world-famous Zane's Cycles," I said.

"How much are you guys asking for a Trek 820?" the caller asked.

"Sir, that model is selling for $269.99," I said, this time with a huge smile on my face. It turned out that this guy had been calling all the bike dealers from A to Z in the phone book and kept getting connected to our line. I guess he was just focused on asking his question and therefore wasn't paying attention each time I picked up the phone and greeted him exactly the same way each time. I bet you can guess where he ended up buying his Trek 820.

In addition to taking advantage of shuttered shops, I've tried, whenever possible, to make it harder for new competitors to enter the market. One example of what we did to implement competitive insulation in our market involved Cycle Madison, which I mentioned previously. That shop was a joint venture I formed with another bike shop owner based in Essex, which was about forty-five minutes east of our shop in Branford. I had heard that Trek was interested in supporting a new shop in the Madison area, a fast-growing suburban neighborhood that is just about halfway between Branford and Essex. Rather than have some new shop owner come in and try to eat both of our lunches, I suggested to my fellow shop owner in Essex that we open up our own shop to serve the Madison market. He agreed and we split the costs of opening the new shop down the middle, which ended up being about $50,000 each.

The nice thing was that I had a sales manager that was looking to move to the Madison area at the time. He was also looking for a new challenge, like managing a shop of his own. So he got the job of managing that shop. And, unlike Zane's, which supplied the recreational crowd, the new shop would cater to the higher-end racing crowd. Our new manager then successfully recruited a mechanic to join him from another one of our competitors and, because both of these guys were well known and trusted by the Trek folks, the company stopped pursuing the idea of opening another shop in the area. Although Cycle Madison is now closed, we kept it running for about seven years so that it could serve its primary purpose: to keep other competitors out of the local market.

I will admit that there are competitors of ours on the national level that I would never want to go toe-to-toe with. I know, for instance, that there are guys running shops in Milwaukee and Portland, Oregon, who I would love to learn a few things from. The goal of competition is to pick off the weaker players and team up with the stronger ones. In fact, a few years down the road, when our national expansion has gathered some steam, perhaps these guys would make great co-branding partners or even full-fledged owners of a joint business. The mistake too many people make about competition is that they let their ego lead them where they don't ever need to go—there is plenty of low-hanging fruit to pick without ever entering into a fight among equals. Of course, the same idea applies in reverse: the stronger I make our business, the crazier someone needs to be to try to enter the market and go toe-to-toe with us. If and when that happens again, we'll be ready.

• tactics for the future •

Obviously, as our corporate rewards division continues to grow like gangbusters and as Zane's starts expanding its retail presence nationally, we'll have even more opportunities to change the rules on our competitors. In chapter ten, I provide more detail about reinventing the wheel and what is required to expand nationally, but suffice it to say that I already have plenty of ideas about some of the things we'll be able to do once Zane's evolves. I continue to learn from my friends at Texas A&M and at Arizona State University who study the impact of superior retailing and customer service. One of the more important findings of their work is that most national businesses consider expenditures on customer service more as sunk costs than as profit drivers. But, the companies that understand that concept and drink the same Kool-Aid that I do, like the grocery chain Stew Leonard's or the home retail shops of The Container Store—both nationally recognized as businesses known for their superior attention to customers—understand that it's an *investment* in long-term success rather than something that can be thought of as a nice-to-have.

You can learn a lot about the values of a company by where it chooses to make its cuts during tough times. Although you might hear about how much a retailer values its customers when times are good, it sure should raise some eyebrows when they lay off most of their frontline staff during the bad times. No matter how bad things get for us, I would spend my very last nickel on those things aimed at building on our customers' experiences. I would cut computers, inventory, and even the size of my store before I cut back on the number of people we needed to make our customers' lives a little better as a result of shopping with us. The cost of connecting with our customers isn't something an accountant can write off as a variable cost—it is a fixed expense and an investment in our future as a business. Without our attention to service, we will lose our differentiation in the market and find ourselves replaced by someone else who understands this principle better than we did.

But, because we do understand this concept, we plan to maximize our prior investments as we look toward the future.

Unlike many other companies who have made the mistake of thinking about service simply as an expense, we have built the foundation of our company on the notion of delivering an exceptional customer experience and we can leverage the strength of that structure as we continue to expand.

As a company on the upswing, we also won't face a lot of the hurdles other national companies might have to overcome in trying to replicate what has made us so successful. Again, we're going to be attacking this game with a fresh set of legs and we're not going to be afraid to reinvent the game entirely if it suits us.

As we roll out nationally, we'll be using our database of some 300,000 customer records to help us pick the best locations for our shops and to seed those areas with the Zane's brand before we've even located there. By sorting the information in that database, we can tell that we already have 200 customers in Phoenix, Arizona, for example, or 75 customers in Denver, Colorado. We can send those folks packets with a Zane's branded T-shirt and water bottle and let them know we're coming so they can tell their friends: soon, you, too, can get lifetime free service just by cycling around the block.

That means, of course, that even though most new businesses might be challenged with a slow start as word gets out about them, we're changing the rules by making sure we'll have momentum as soon as we hit the ground. Again, as long as we stick to our mission of delivering unique experiences to our customers, it doesn't matter what playing field we land on—look out below!

· 7 ·

focus on continuous improvement

WE HAVE TALKED at length to this point about all the things we already do well that make up Zane's Cycles. But we are always on the hunt for new and better ways to serve our corporate customers, as well as those that walk into our retail stores. That's why we are constantly interacting with our customers at different levels in a never-ending effort to come up with new ideas and practices that will help engage each and every one of them at an emotional level. We are constantly striking up conversations or sending out surveys and asking for feedback on how we might be able to do things even better than we already are. The truth is that as soon as we sit back and relax, thinking we have everything figured out, some-one else will likely devise a way to steal our customers from under our noses.

> The simple act of asking your customers to rate your service—and, just as important, acting on the information that you receive—is an extremely effective way of making the changes to your service or product offerings for which your customers are begging.

One example of how we acted upon direct feedback from our customers was the changes we made in schedul-ing our service calls. Every week, particularly in the warmer months, we get hundreds of bikes dropped off for a variety of servicing—everything from tune-ups to wheel align-ments and other repairs. Because of all that volume, we had adopted a policy where customers could expect to get back their bikes within two weeks after they had dropped them off with us.

It soon became clear, however, that the policy simply wasn't good enough. Understandably, many customers didn't want to wait that long before their next ride. Listen-ing to that feedback led us to modify the policy dramati-cally: any bike that was dropped off by the close of business on Monday (6:30 P.M.) could be picked back up on Friday of that week. Any bike received on Tuesday or later would then be ready on Sunday or the following Monday. In listening to our customers, we realized that most of them ride their bikes on the weekends and that as long as we had their bike ready before Saturday, they'd be happy as clams.

Of course, acknowledging the feedback was easy; doing something about it was obviously more difficult. Once we made the commitment to turning our repairs around in a week, that meant we needed to stand by it. As a result, we began paying our mechanics overtime wages whenever we had to in order to make good on the promises we had made to our customers. At the same time, we also learned from talking to some customers during particularly busy weeks that they did not, in fact, need their bike that week: they were headed out of town for the weekend or simply weren't in a rush to get it back. These customers understood our policy and, rather than taking the whole bowl of quarters we were offering them, they were willing to work with us to help us meet our other commitments. By creating a triage of sorts using the information about who really needed their bikes earlier, we could then shift around our service calls, prioritizing those repairs we needed to get done first, which not only kept us on schedule but also cut down on the overtime we needed to rack up to get it done.

Another example of how we turned customer feedback into action was when we began offering free installation for any roof rack system our customers purchased. Roof rack systems, which sell for three hundred to four hundred complete, are among our best-selling items. But, even as our customers are ringing up their purchase, you can tell they're already a little bit apprehensive about taking it out of the box and installing it on the roof of their car. If you aren't familiar with putting one of these racks together, which are sold by vendors like Yakima or Thule, the installation can be somewhat tricky because of the number of small and intricate parts involved. Although the instructions that come with the racks are typically excellent, you need to be willing to follow the instructions carefully step by step. Just like if you're putting together a piece of furniture you bought at Ikea, if you miss a step or skip anything, you'll have to start all over again.

As we listened to our customers asking for help in putting these racks together, we decided we'd offer an optional free installation. "Throw the rack in your trunk and try to put it together at home if you want," we tell our customers as they are checking out. "And if you run into any problems, leave all the parts in the trunk, call us up to schedule an appointment, and we'll get it ready for you in under an hour. Or, if you want to avoid the hassle altogether, let's find a time when we can install it for you right now."

The amazing thing about this program is that it had two huge benefits. One, it gave customers a comfort level in buying the racks because they didn't have to worry about installing them anymore. Two, by offering the free installation service, we never have to discount our racks to move them— our customers are willing to pay the full price in order to get access to the service. That adds up to a win-win scenario for everyone. Let's say the installation might take a half hour for one of my mechanics to complete. Given that I pay him twenty dollars an hour, the cost of that service to us is about ten dollars. But, we come out ahead anyway because I don't have to knock 10 percent off the price tag, which would have cost us thirty to forty dollars, to sell the rack. In other words, it pays to talk to your customers so that you can learn the things they truly value about what you're offering them. Our goal is to sweep our customers off their feet so that they end up thanking us for giving them more than they expected to receive.

Each and every customer who walks in the door of one of our shops has the potential to give us a piece of feedback that will help us boost the quality of our service an extra notch or so, with the goal of doing something else to keep our offering unique in the marketplace. That's why the thing we prioritize most with anyone who works at Zane's is that he or she will need to engage our customers on a personal level as quickly as possible. We want customers to get an immediate and genuine sense that they matter to us.

One of the advantages of working in the retail business is that you as the retailer have countless opportunities to engage your customers on a one-to-one basis. This is where our customer database proves so helpful. Rather than allowing each customer to remain nameless, we ask customers to remind us of their last names and look up their shopping history with us. Then, we can steer our conversations toward the kinds of bikes or merchandise our customers really want to learn about rather than wasting time hashing over things they already have or know about.

For instance, if a customer who walks in hasn't been to one of our stores in months, we can begin by asking her if her bike happens to be hanging on her car rack out in the parking lot. If so, we can suggest that she bring it in so we can tune it up. Or, we might ask how the bike is working out and whether there might be something we could adjust to make it more comfortable for that customer to get out riding more regularly. On the other hand, if the customer you're working with happens to be a regular who stops in to the shop every week or two, she is clearly an enthusiast and may either want to talk about buying something for an upcoming ride or even about the choices for upgrading her bike.

We're also enhancing our database technology to create a seamless nationwide network as part of our national rollout. Then, simply by using a last name and a phone number, we can access each customer's history, regardless of what store or corporate rewards program she received her bike from. We'll also be giving our people on the sales floor mobile PDAs, which are essentially 7-inch laptops, that they can use to access all that information to help speed the introduction between themselves and the customers. Again, the point is to find ways to make the most of those twenty-five minutes we have to find a connection with that customer.

• make your intentions clear •

Certainly, we do get asked from time to time about why we collect so much information from our customers; after all, everybody's just a bit worried about their personal data floating around these days. You never know when someone might steal your identity and order you a bike, right? We tell our customers up front that our goal in collecting that information is to find ways to serve our customers better than we did on their last visit.

Think about the classic example of what *not* to do, a story starring Radio Shack. For years, every time you bought something from a Radio Shack, the first thing the clerk ringing up your purchase would say was, "Phone number, please." The amazing thing was that even if you asked that clerk why they needed a phone number, you only received a blank look in return, along with a lame excuse such as, "I can't do anything on the computer until I put the number in." It was worse than talking to a parrot.

I might have understood why they wanted the number if I ever received any coupons in the mail or an alert to an upcoming sale, but it seems that Radio Shack never truly did *anything* with that phone number. So why make your customer uncomfortable by even asking for it? Radio Shack clearly came to understand this as well because its staff no longer asks for a number. (Unfortunately, sales clerks seem to have replaced it with "Do you want to buy a cell phone?"— a question I've been asked far too many times—even though I'm typing out a text message or leaving a message via the phone in my hand while they're asking it. Talk about employees on autopilot.)

At Zane's, we proactively engage our customers in a conversation where we explain how giving us their contact information has less to do with benefiting us but far more to do with benefiting them. By creating a customer account with us, he or she will never have to worry about saving a receipt in case they want to return something because we'll have it all in our computer. We'll also use that information to keep track of product recalls. What we'll never do is sell that information or put it at risk. In fact, if the fire alarm in our store goes off, I'm leaving the safe and grabbing the computer because our customer database is the most valuable asset we have.

The key, though, is not to let that information die on the vine—you have to do something with it. Quite frankly, we consider it a benefit for our customers that we're not going to waste their time talking about things or services they have already bought. We'd rather spend our face-to-face time talking about what they want to discuss. Knowing what our customers have bought from us in the past always gives us the chance to ask questions like, "How's that new pump working out?" Or, "Everything riding better after that last tune-up we did for you?" It's by asking these questions that we usually get our most valuable feedback because it's often specific to a product or service we're offering—and that's information we can turn into action.

• always ask, "what can we do better?" •

Of course, because of our work in shipping bikes on behalf of our corporate customers, we don't always have the opportunity to meet the recipients of our bikes face-to-face. As a result, we have increasingly turned to surveying our customers to get some insight into what all of them—those from our retail shop as well as those corporate recipients— think about Zane's, even if they're not standing in one of our shops. Asking the question "What can we do better?" is actually the core of taking a customer-centric approach to any business. And with today's technology, like the Internet, e-mail, and database management, surveying has never been easier. In fact, feel free to visit www.zanes.com to see the latest version of our own survey posted on our site. We say as a greeting, "At Zane's Cycles, your feedback matters! Please be as open and as candid as possible. Your honesty will allow us to identify and improve upon any weaknesses, so that we may serve you better."

The ultimate goal of conducting these surveys is, of course, to find out how to further cement our relationships with our customers, either by implementing new ideas or modifying existing practices that might be ineffective or unpopular. We get thousands of responses every month, from both our customers at the retail shop and those that we service on behalf of our corporate clients like Tropicana and American Express.

For every bike we deliver, we ask customers to rank our service on a scale of one to ten on questions like: "Did the bike show up when we said it would?" or, "Was your bike in the condition we said it would be in?" (And, just to give those customers an extra incentive to respond, we raffle off a bike to one lucky respondent every month.)

> Although many companies claim to survey their customers, I believe that most fail to deliver on a key element: actually doing something with the feedback they receive. We don't just send out these surveys for show; we use the results to let our customers point the way in how we can service them better than we did the day before.

Although many companies claim to survey their customers, I believe that most fail to deliver on a key element: actually doing something with the feedback they receive. We don't just send out these surveys for show; we use the results to let our customers point the way in how we can service them better than we did the day before. It is unbelievably more powerful to make additions or changes to any business's offering if that charge is being led by the voices of customers rather than just some bright ideas dreamed up by the MBAs with management titles.

For example, we have made fourteen procedural changes in how we deliver our bikes on behalf of our corporate clients based solely on information we picked up from surveys completed by the recipients of our bikes. Many of these changes were driven by complaints we received that revolved around damages that occurred to the bikes from the time we put them into a truck until they arrived at the recipient's home. So, we reexamined every aspect of how we packed our bikes and changed everything from the kind of packing material we used to wrap around the frames to the kinds of zip ties and elastic bands we used to keep the bike's parts from shifting during transit.

Although we assemble 100 percent of the bike in our shops, we're forced to take a few things apart, like the pedals, so that the bike will fit into a uniform shipping box. We just used to stuff the assembly instructions into one of the bags containing loose parts like the pedals. But, as an extra precaution in case those bags were lost during shipping or mistakenly left out of the box, we began stapling the assembly instructions to the packaging padding the frame of the bike. Because the instructions also included a checklist of what should be included in the box, customers wouldn't have to beat on their heads wondering if we had left some crucial part or tool out.

One of the most common complaints we heard, something we would get hundreds of phone calls on each month, was customers telling us they were confused about how to screw the pedals back onto their bikes. The problem was that, even though we included instructions with photos that showed how to reassemble the bike, we still hadn't done enough when it came to explaining how the pedals worked. With different thread directions for left and right pedals, and it can be confusing for anyone who isn't a bike mechanic to know which is which. We'd get calls to our service center that went something like, "The pedals you shipped me are stripped." That wasn't the case. The solution was that it was necessary to twist the left-hand side pedal in the opposite direction of the right-hand side pedal to tighten it. We pondered how to solve this problem for a while before we came up with an answer. The solution was stickers that showed which direction the pedal needed to be turned to screw it in. After we stuck color-coded left and right arrows on the pedals and cranks, all the customers had to do was match them up and turn them in the appropriate direction. Problem solved. Total cost: about a penny apiece.

Not only did we help our customers get out riding sooner than they could before we brought out the stickers, we accomplished a bit of cost- and time-saving for ourselves. If you consider that when we receive a customer call to discuss this very problem, one of my mechanics might spend at least fifteen minutes a pop: five minutes to let the customer detail the problem, five minutes to explain the solution, and then another five minutes to wait on the line to make sure the customer successfully completes the assembly. No more—we eliminated thousands of hours of phone time for a mere $100 worth of stickers—all thanks to listening and acting upon the direct input from our customers.

As technology like the Internet has become more widespread and accessible to everyone, we have also recently expanded our use of these new high-tech tools to help head off or solve problems brought to us by our customers. Whenever someone orders one of our bikes from their corporate rewards program, for instance, we send them an e-mail directing them to our Web site, where they can enter their height, inseam, and other measurements so that we can custom-fit their bike perfectly. We used to have customers fax their information in, but as technology privacy issues have become more prevalent, we now use a secure server to collect that information quickly and securely online.

After the order has been placed, recipients receive a reply e-mail acknowledging that we have successfully processed their entry (which eliminated another couple hundred phone calls a month from folks wondering if we had received their information), and also containing a tracking number they could use to follow the progress of their bikes from our shop to their home. Most recently, we also added a link back to our Web site within the body of that e-mail so our customers can now access a nine-minute-long online video where I walk them through each step in the assembly of their bike after they receive it. We spent two days on a sound stage in New Hampshire recording the video, which was then spruced up and edited into its current form. Because each of our bikes, regardless of the model, needs the same kind of assembly to get it out on the road or trail, the video, which customers can access anytime and as many times as they want or need to, has proven to be helpful in heading off customer problems. Perhaps more important, it has also given us yet another unique way to connect on an emotional level with our customers.

Even though the material is incredibly helpful in alleviating the insecurity of a nonmechanically inclined recipient, we get the most feedback on the blooper segments we include—who doesn't love bloopers, right? Well, apparently our customers like them more than the regular videos themselves, which is fine by me because it clearly shows that we have yet another way to cement that emotional connection with our customers.

The results of our surveys also play a critical role in building better relationships with our corporate clients as well. The fact that we survey our customers at all, in fact, helps differentiate us from our competition. Whenever I meet up with clients like Marriott or American Express, I bring along a stack of about 500 printed survey results, which stands about three inches tall. In fact, whenever we land a new corporate partner, I get a kick out of thumping that huge stack of paper down on my liaison's desk. The reaction I usually get, though, is: "What the heck am I supposed to do with these?" My standard answer is, "I'm giving you these results to prove that we're representing your brand, as well as Zane's, as well as we can. And I'm not just saying that—the proof is in these results." I remind my clients that Zane's is, after all, working on their behalf to deliver an award, a brand-new bike, to one of their own prized customers. I want my client to know how well we are doing in that regard. And, unlike my competition, I want to document how well we're doing with stories and information delivered directly from our mutual customers.

"My goal," I tell my clients, "is to make sure that your phone doesn't ring with a complaint from a recipient regarding anything about their bike—like that it might be the wrong size or they don't know how to attach the pedals. We're creating an emotional bond between you and your customers by doing our job as well as we possibly can." To say this another way, by using surveys to back our word, we uncovered yet another way to energize the relationship with our clients. Finding these points of differentiation is absolutely critical if you want to ensure that you're the only one your clients think of when it comes time to renew your contract with them.

• win back at-risk customers •

One of the goals of sending out surveys is also to work on identifying how you can retain your customers, which is often far more cost-effective than simply trying to win new ones. But it can often be a tricky notion to determine which of your customers might be at the most risk of switching their allegiances to one of your competitors. That's why one of the more interesting articles I came across about the time I sat down to write this book was a piece in the *Harvard Business Review* in which a few researchers dug into a long-held myth about customer surveys. As I mentioned earlier, when we send out surveys, we ask our customers to rate how well we are doing using a scale from one to ten. Most companies use this classic one-to-ten scale, where customers can choose a nine or a ten to show they were extremely satisfied with the service they received, a seven or an eight to show they were satisfied, and anything below a seven meant the customer was either indifferent or unhappy with the product or service they were rating.

That *HBR* article attacked the logic that companies should focus their marketing and retention efforts on those customers who reported scores in the one to six range; the customers you really need to be focused on are the sevens and eights, the researchers found. Although those customers say they are currently satisfied by the services they are receiving, their scores also indicate that if someone better came along, they'd switch in a minute.

This was an eye-opening thought for me. I started thinking about how I might rate some of the businesses I used regularly, such as my dry cleaner, coffee shop, or even my accountant and lawyer. I knew I would give my lawyer and accountants solid tens—there was no way I would switch to someone else. But there is some wiggle room when it comes to some of the other businesses I frequent. For example, even though I would give my dry cleaner an eight because he always does a decent enough job (except for the one expensive tie he lost), if someone better came along, someone offering a unique or interesting service, I would definitely switch things up. The same goes for the coffee shop where I stop in on my way to the office.

When I translated these thoughts into what they meant for Zane's, I knew we had to make some changes in how we dealt with our survey results. The customers who were giving us a seven or an eight, folks who I used to consider solidly in our camp, might, in fact, be vulnerable to our competition. That meant we needed to spend just as much and perhaps more effort in turning our sevens and eights into nines and tens as we did on moving our twos and threes up the ladder.

I also came across another interesting study that was discussed at one of our industry trade shows a few years back. The study's results found that the primary reason customers switched between offerings was not because of price, selection, or even the quality of the service they had received—it was because they felt the business they were leaving was indifferent to them. In other words, there was simply no emotional connection between that person and the business. Whenever customers walk into a store and are ignored by the sales staff or made to feel insignificant, they will automatically be at risk for looking for someone else who will make them feel as if they matter.

That's why store managers like Tom are constantly combing through our database to track down customers that we haven't heard from in a while. Tom will actually call up these customers and ask them to stop by the shop and bring in their bikes for a free tune-up so we can make sure everything is still working well on the bike. We want to remind the customer that we truly value him or her and we're willing to go the extra mile to prove it. It is also why we spend so much effort on training our sales staff to interact with our customers on as deep a level as possible. One example is that part of the job requirement for each of our sales team members is to send a handwritten thank-you note to any customer who buys a bike from us. Purchasing a bike isn't like buying a DVD player at Walmart. We want to find a personalized way to acknowledge that to our customers—to thank them for choosing us.

I remember one time when a woman who had just bought a bike from me said, "You don't have to send me a thank-you card; I already have two." I ended up sending her another two: one to her home and another to work.

No, I wasn't trying to be annoying, just proving a point: this is simply what we do at Zane's. Any time we can show how we're delivering extra value to our customers, the better chance we have of making that emotional connection with them that will turn them from sevens and eights into tens.

But, as important as it is to invest in our at-risk customers, I also recognize that my competitors probably have no idea which of their customers are actually at risk of leaving. As they spend their resources trying to win back their really unhappy customers, we actually have the opportunity to win their sevens and eights away from them. Recognizing that there is a large pool of customers out there just waiting to be plucked has been an "A-ha!" moment for us at Zane's. These are the folks that ride their bikes enough to frequent their neighborhood bike shop, a place they feel does a pretty good job for them. But, if we got the chance to invite these same riders into our shop, we would simply blow them away with all the extra advantages we offer our customers.

Simply put, our competitors have helped us by setting low expectation levels for these customers. All we have to do is show them all the aspects that make our service stand out and we can instantly acquire an army of newly loyal customers in a heartbeat at a far lower cost than trying to attract customers new to the sport. The fact that my competitors fail to understand this and continue to sleep soundly, blowing their limited resources on acquiring new customers while thinking their sevens and eights are loyal customers, makes the equation all the sweeter for us.

• bottom up, not top down •

When we think about where Zane's is headed into the future, as we go national and beyond, I can guarantee that we'll be listening to our customers and letting them help us head down the best path for our organization. I like to say that we're a bottom-up rather than a top-down organization, which means that the best information to turn into action usually comes from our customers along with those employees who interact most with those customers, as opposed to making decisions based solely on the input from management or academics sealed in ivory towers that make their recommendations and grand proclamations in a vacuum.

The key balance we've found is that by working with scholars with their feet on the ground like Martin Mende and Len Berry, and all the great folks at ASU's Center for Service Leadership (too many to name), we can put textbook theories to the test by letting our frontline people experiment with them and amplify them by applying their own out-of-the-big-box skills. I have to admit that in my younger days, I was skeptical about any academic—you know the old saying, "Those who cannot do, teach." Well, today I can admit how helpful it is to get input about new ideas from people who can think objectively because they remain above the daily fray. The key for us has been to take the theories and transform them into actions that not only validate the theories but empower everyone in our organization to do our jobs—delivering unique experiences—

better than we ever have before. The acid test for me has always been—if my people believe in it, it can work.

> I have to admit that in my younger days, I was skeptical about any academic...today I can admit how helpful it is to get input about new ideas from people who can think objectively because they remain above the daily fray.
>
> The key for us has been to take the theories and transform them into actions that not only validate the theories but empower everyone in our organization to do our jobs—delivering unique experiences—better than we ever have before.

When I tell people outside the company about this philosophy, I often receive a chuckle or a smirk in return, along with a snide comment like, "Sure, Chris, whatever you say. Every big company says the same thing these days." I let those comments roll right off me because I know that Zane's is unique in what we do and that we don't have the same kinds of barriers to overcome that other bigger companies that claim to be customer-centric are forced to deal with. We have built Zane's from the ground up on the sole premise that our success is 100 percent tied to our ability to listen and then act upon what our customers are asking us to do.

This fact also lends itself as a kind of segue into the topic we'll talk about in the next chapter—how you can tailor your hiring decisions to make your organization even more effective at listening and responding to the needs of your customers.

· 8 ·

hiring help

WHEN IT COMES to making decisions on adding new members to our team, I've come to recognize that the best employee is not necessarily someone who racks up the most sales—it's the employee who is most committed to doing something friendly and unexpected for our customers. And, for the same reason, I don't necessarily want to hire employees simply because they are fanatical bikers either—a hard-core rider might be turned off by the questions of a new customer or inadvertently steer that customer toward buying equipment he'll never need.

· · ·

My goal is to build a team of people who have both the aptitude to learn the nuances of riding and the ability to translate those details for our customers. I can always teach someone about the "ins and outs" of bikes, but I can't teach someone to have empathy and kindness for our customers and toward his or her co-workers as well. My main criteria in adding new members to our team is, "Is this person intrinsically nice?"

• recruit nice people who have • the potential to deliver great service

Think about what it's like to go to your auto mechanic. The guy (and, unfortunately, it is a guy most of the time) can make you wince with just a glance or a mutter after you've dropped off your car. Although you couldn't help hoping that the rattle you've been hearing or that "Check Engine" light wasn't really a problem, the look on your mechanic's face quickly dashes all your hopes.

"Oh boy," you say to yourself. "How much is this going to cost me?" Inevitably, you're told that some critical part in your car has failed. But, lucky for you, your mechanic will take care of it for you at a cost of several hundred dollars. Granted, most mechanics know their trade inside and out and, at the end of the day, your car will get fixed. But, if you dare ask a question about why that important-sounding cog needs to be replaced, well, you'll get a lot of meaningless garage take, leaving you with no choice but to nod your head and open your wallet. To me, that's a broken business model; it should be flipped around. The customer should be the one with the power to ask the questions and get answers that mean something to him or her.

At Zane's, we're not a technical company—as I keep emphasizing, we're in the experience business. Providing the best possible experiences to our customers means that we need to have people in place who are willing to answer patiently every question a customer might have. That's why we hire fun, upbeat, and self-confident men and women of all ages who actually enjoy interacting with our customers. I believe that a person's degree of self-confidence is a strong barometer of how that person will interact with other staff and customers. These kinds of folks are secure in who they are, whereas insecure people tend to have chips on their shoulders that keep them from stepping beyond their comfort zone.

We have guys and gals working for us that are simply the best bike mechanics around—that's their niche, and they know their skills are important. But if they can't also interact with our customers, Zane's doesn't have a use for them. We want employees whose skills are more than one dimensional. The same rule applies to big-time riders who read all the cycling magazines and invest half their paycheck in buying new frames, wheels, and gadgets every year. Although I love to strike up a conversation with guys like this, I'm not sure I want them trying to sell bikes to the family of four that just walked in the door. Sometimes, these riders can acquire a bit of arrogance about the kind of gear they ride with—

and they can look down upon those of us who simply don't measure up to their requirements. The family of four has far different needs in terms of the bikes they want to buy than what this guy is interested in. Although my fanatical friend might be willing to pay a premium for the lightweight, ultra-fast road bikes he rides every day after work, the family is probably more interested in hybrid bikes they can ride both on the road and on the nearest rail trail on the weekend. Ideally, I'm looking for enthusiastic and curious people who can find ways to connect with both the weekend riders and the die-hards in an effort to convert them into lifetime customers.

• the power of pointing north •

Sometimes, even a Zane's customer can push too far, perhaps by trying to tip more than the whole bowl of quarters into his or her pocket. Worse, perhaps a would-be customer even goes so far as to take a test ride on one of our bikes and never turns back—it happens.

In fact, every year we lose about five bikes during a test ride. Inevitably, the employee who was working with these thieves that pose as customers is embarrassed and wants to do something about it, often first jumping into his or her car to try to track down the culprit.

More than once, I've also had staffers come up to me suggesting that we should start a new policy where we take the potential customer's keys or their driver's license before he or she takes out a $350 bike. But most customers are blown away by how much we trust them and that goes far in building their confidence in us. As soon as we begin distrusting our customers and treating them like potential thieves, we'll automatically be putting our relationship in jeopardy. We simply cannot begin creating new standard operating procedures that don't meet that one critical goal. Sure, we may lose those five bikes a year, but the other 4,995 that are test ridden do return. That said, it's not as if I condone theft, and whenever we can catch a thief red-handed, I'm all for it (see the sidebar on page 163 for an example in which we did just that).

When faced with these sorts of circumstances, the key for any Zane's employee is to be flexible and, above all, not to overreact. To that point, we have a mantra that goes, "Point North." In essence, this slogan gives everyone on our team a baseline to rely on when things begin to go wrong. I came up with this concept during one of my speeches when I asked everyone in attendance to first close their eyes and then to point in the direction they thought was north. Then, after everyone opened his or her eyes, we could all have a chuckle because just about everyone was pointing in a different direction.

For everyone who works at Zane's, "Point North" literally means a fixed point in the north end of the shop, where we have a plaque that reads, "The only difference between us and our competition is the service that we offer," along with a little shrine of sorts that has our goal, mission, and laws of winning lifetime customers printed on it. Rather than everyone pointing in different directions or wondering how they should react when a customer acts in a way we'd prefer they didn't, that sign, like the North Star for sailors, works as a compass and gives us a constant point of reference to keep us on track with our core message.

Whenever we see one of our co-workers struggling to see eye to eye with a customer over a $20 return, showing the customer the kind of body language that says, "Hey, buddy, quit trying to take advantage of us," that's our cue to swing by and whisper in his or her ear: "Point North." Uttering those words is a reminder about why we're here: to win that $12,500 lifetime relationship, not to prove this customer wrong today. Not everyone can embrace this concept, though; it takes a degree of emotional maturity and a sense of self to have the ability to think about someone else's point of view.

When we look at unfortunate scenarios involving thieves—both those posing as customers and those trying to pass themselves off as loyal employees—we need to balance our message that we are customer-centric with the notion that we are willing to take a stand against anyone who puts our organization at risk. Those that play by the rules will be treated like kings and queens; those that don't, well, let's say that we tend to hold grudges. The point is that we won't overregulate our customers based on a few bad apples. But we will make an example of anyone who takes advantage of our generosity.

I once chased down a kid who stole a set of red aluminum valve caps. Even though the caps, which are extremely

· to catch a thief ·

A few years ago, a young guy took out a bike to test ride it, but one of my employees saw him make a hard turn out of the shop and start riding fast down Route 1, which runs right in front of our Branford building. Strangely enough, the employee who saw the guy taking off called up his father, who happened to be a fireman at the Branford Fire Department, which also just happened to be in the path of our would-be thief.

"Someone just stole one of our bikes," our guy yelled into the phone. "We need some help!"

I guess the station scrambled because as soon as that guy rode in front of the fire station, five firemen jumped out and tackled him into the grass. It was like something out of a cop show! After we got our bike back, we prosecuted the guy to the fullest extent of the law. It gives everyone on the team a tremendous lift knowing that we protect our reputation and make an example of injustice to Zane's with the same passion we have concerning the relationship with our customers.

popular with BMX riders looking to color-coordinate their bikes, were probably worth only about three dollars, I called the cops and had that kid arrested. Given that he was a juvenile under the age of sixteen, I knew he wouldn't go to jail, but I needed to make an example out of him so that his friends didn't start thinking that Zane's was an easy mark. I was more than vindicated in my decision when the kid's father stopped in to the store not long after the incident to thank me for teaching his son a valuable lesson.

Unfortunately, I have also had to go to similar lengths with employees from time to time, most recently when two now-former employees decided it was a good idea to steal several Nintendo Wii systems from us and then sell them on the Internet. These fellas are now sitting in jail and looking at felonies for their stupidity.

We will bend over backward to make the lives of our customers and our employees easier—after all, we all thrive in trusting environments where you know you will find support. But, once you cross us, the rules change. Although we might be able to afford $2,000 in losses a year, we can't afford $20,000, so if we do make a mistake in trusting someone, we will do our best to make sure we correct it in the most deliberate way possible.

• keep your eyes and ears open for talent •

So, what's reinventing the wheel at Zane's in terms of finding these fun and self-confident people we keep referring to? One thing we don't do is place ads online or in newspapers. This approach, in my opinion, would actually be the worst thing we could do. We'd get a lot of responses, but we wouldn't have any good way to filter the wheat from the chaff. We'd end up interviewing far too many knuckle-heads. The truth is that some of our best employees actually began as customers or as friends of those customers. It's helpful to keep a database of relationships in your head, remembering names from today that might be ready to fill jobs tomorrow.

If we meet someone that would fit within the Zane's culture, it's well worth the effort to remember that person, even if we might not have an open position to fill at that time. When you do find good people, they can then connect you to their network of similarly valuable friends and family. We're also always on the lookout for those people who have that special blend of character and personality that will lead to some real chemistry with our team at Zane's—people that you just know are capable of making positive connections with our customers. If one of our employees tells Tom or me that one of our customers could be a good fit for our team, one of us will go over and chat them up and, if we're impressed, we'll often offer a job right there in the middle of the store. Of course, because we're offering jobs to lawyers, business owners, and university professors, they often politely decline. But, every once in a while, we find someone that might be in between jobs or just happens to be looking to try something different with their career for a while.

We've also been lucky to be referred to some of our best employees through other employees or even through our business partners. I wound up hiring Tom, who has seventeen years experience and is now my most senior employee, after the folks at Trek tipped me off to him.

At the time, Tom was working for another bike shop about an hour away from our Branford shop and I had been hearing rumors of this hotshot kid who brought something special to his customers. At the same time, my retail manager happened to be moving away to Colorado and I was hunting around for his replacement. The same Trek representative (who, by the way, was the roommate of my exiting manager) serviced our shop and the one Tom was working at and, after seeing the similarities between Tom and me, recommended that I make some time to talk to him.

At first, I was reluctant because the last thing I wanted to do was steal an employee from another Trek shop. But, as it turned out, Tom was ready for a change. I used to trade inventory from time to time with the shop Tom worked at, and we would often hop into a car and deliver bikes to each other. One day, Tom showed up to pick up a bike he had asked for on behalf of one of his customers. Taking advantage of the situation, I bought him a coffee and talked about all the ideas I had about how we could run the store. I even told him that I thought he'd be the perfect guy to help me get there.

"I've heard great things about you from the folks at Trek," I told him. "They seem to think we'd make a great team. What do you think?"

He told me he was flattered, but that he needed to sleep on it. He called me up a day or two later and said, "Chris,

I'm ready for something new and I like what you've told me—count me in." The rest is history; Zane's wouldn't be where it is today without Tom's contributions over the years.

• empower your employees •

Once we've attracted top-notch and nice employees onto the Zane's team, and coached them in the "Point North" philosophy, the next key step is to empower them with the ability to think and act for themselves. As we grow Zane's from a single shop into a national chain of stores, this becomes more important than ever. That's where the power of "Point North" can help, but it also means managers like me have to rid ourselves of the habit of micromanaging everyone working on our team. If you're going to invest in hiring the best people, you need to be able to trust them to make snap decisions without first floating every option up the chain of command. Every employee needs to have the ability to dole out the bowl of quarters in the pursuit of pleasing our customers.

Our children's trade-up bike program, for instance, was Tom's idea and he had the power to make it work. Another example happened a few years ago when Tom told me that the staff was burned out from a busy summer and that he wanted to close the shop a few hours early so he could take everyone to a local amusement park.

I'll admit, my first reaction was something like, "Uh, Tom, it's the middle of July, one of our busiest months—are you nuts?" But I trusted Tom with the decision and, as usual, it was the right one. We ended up putting up a note on the front door that said "Closed for Bastille Day," a little joke in that it was purely coincidental that our unplanned holiday fell on July 14. We also posted a note to our customers that said, in consideration of the inconvenience we might have caused them for closing early, we would give them a 10 percent discount off their next purchase if they mentioned the note. Not only did Tom's idea rejuvenate the staff, the customers that came in to claim their discount seemed to get a kick out of the whole experience. As a result, our "Bastille Day" excursion has now become an annual event.

But employees also need to be accountable for their mission to deliver an extraordinary experience to our customers. Everything else is secondary. As soon as a customer walks in the door, everything else—from stocking shelves to vacuuming the floor—should stop so that we can give our customer our undivided attention. Any employee that doesn't get that concept won't be working for Zane's for very long. One of my pet peeves is finding people who put themselves on what I like to call "autopilot" when they're working. By this, I mean people who aren't engaged in what they're doing and, as a result, tend to turn off their brains. Take, for example, the employee who mindlessly overnights a package, paying the hefty extra fee to do so, when there was no need to expedite the shipment—regular postage would have been fine. Or the office manager who just buys copy paper off the shelf rather than searching the Internet for a better buy. Although these might seem like minor examples, they show me that someone isn't using his or her brain for the benefit of the organization.

I expect each and every employee to have a reason for an action they take. Nothing raises my ire quite as much as when I ask one of my employees why he or she did something, and I get a deer in the headlights response like "I don't know" in reply. Not only is that answer not good enough when I hear it from one of my kids, it's unacceptable in the workplace. I'm far less concerned about the result of the decision or action employees make as long as they used the customer experience as the yardstick in taking their action.

One telling example of this concept in action occurred on a trip I took with my family to Boston to see a Red Sox game. With all the traveling I do, I have become a preferred member of Hilton, so that's where we chose to stay on our excursion in Beantown. Although we had a great time at the game, things took a decided turn for the worse when I got a knock on my door at eight thirty the following morning, followed by the announcement of "Housekeeping." Housekeeping? At eight thirty on a Tuesday morning? I wasn't pleased—didn't they know we hadn't even checked out yet? I was annoyed enough with the experience to throw on some clothes and head down to the front desk, where I asked for the manager. After explaining what had happened, I asked that he comp my room.

At first, he took a second to process what I asking. Then, he apologized for our inconvenience and asked me why I thought I should get my room for free. Bad move on his part. That led me to get even more upset as I explained that the whole point of staying in a hotel is to sleep. And yet, I hadn't been allowed to. "I'm sure there were dozens of rooms where the guest had already checked out because it was a weekday and business travelers usually have meetings in the morning," I said. "But why had the maid been sent to our room when we were clearly still in it?" He told me the hotel wasn't equipped to coordinate between the maid service and the checkouts at the front desk and my room was probably next to the housekeeping closet. I told him that wasn't a good enough answer. Furthermore, I told this manager how often I stayed at Hilton hotels all over the world. Unless he comped my room, I would be giving my business to a rival hotel and Hilton would lose me as a lifetime customer, a fact I would make clear in a letter I would be sending to the hotel's management team. As I wound down, the manager finally got it: "No problem, Mr. Zane, your room is comped—again, I apologize for the inconvenience."

At a certain point, this manager was skilled enough to realize that I was indeed a regular customer and that, for the cost of one night's lodging, he could salvage our relationship. I wasn't asking for five nights in a Caribbean hotel—all I wanted was one free night. Fortunately, this manager was empowered to make that decision without having to risk further alienating me by checking with his own boss. He was also listening to me to learn exactly what he needed to do to win me back. The lesson learned was that each and every employee should be counted on to do what needs to be done to rescue a customer relationship.

• the valentine's day massacre •

As highly as I think of Tom and of the entire Zane's team, not everyone is above making a mistake. When things go wrong, the key is to turn the experience into something positive in terms of evaluating an employee's potential because it's when the chips are down that most people show their true character. One of the stories that we've repeated the most over the years involves a mistake involving an unfortunate customer, a couple of great employees, and a case study in how to win back an angry customer that I've come to call the Valentine's Day Massacre.

> When things go wrong, the key is to turn the experience into something positive in terms of evaluating an employee's potential because it's when the chips are down that most people show their true character.

It all began a week or two before Valentine's Day 2001. A female customer, let's call her Sue, had come into the shop to buy a bicycle for her husband, Bob, as a gift for the holiday. Because she had gone all out to get the very best bike she could for her husband, Sue had put down a deposit on the bike until she could save up the remaining $200 to pay it off. But, until then, and to really blow her husband away, she was going to wrap the bike in some ribbon and attach a few helium balloons to the handlebars along with a big sign that read, "Happy Valentine's Day, Bob." She then asked one of my employees, Greg Ciocci, if he could put the bike in the display window that evening. Sue and Bob were planning on going out to dinner that evening and she planned to drive by the store to surprise her husband with his gift.

Greg, of course, said "No problem." He was happy to help pull off the surprise. At this point, everyone in the store had heard about the plan and all of us couldn't wait to hear how excited Bob was when he saw his new bike later that night. Everything was in place, except for the simple fact that Greg (and Tom, for that matter) forgot all about it. The bike remained in the back of the shop, locked up in Tom's office, until the next morning. I can only imagine how terrible Sue felt when, after dropping hints along the way about what she might have bought, she pulled up in front of the shop later that night. After prodding Bob out of the car, Sue told him to go look in the window. Doing as he was told, Bob peered in to see . . . nothing. Valentine's Day 2001 had become a disaster—we had killed Cupid.

I received a voice mail message from an irate Sue the next morning. I could tell she was basically in tears or at least had been crying for some time as she related everything that had gone wrong. I called up Tom and we worked out a game plan. Somehow, we needed to turn Sue from a potential terrorist into an apostle. To do that, we knew we needed to pull out all the stops and somehow turn this disaster into a positive experience for Sue and Bob. What should we do? First off, Tom suggested, we should deliver the bike to Sue and Bob's home that evening and write off the remaining balance she owed on the bike. We should also try to re-create a romantic evening to replace the one we clearly ruined, so I called up Quattro's, the best Italian restaurant in the area, and made arrangements for Sue and Bob to have their meal on us, with the stipulation that there would be no spending limit. As a final token of our apology, I called up Cilantro's, a gourmet coffee shop up the road, and ordered up an elaborate catered lunch for Sue and her co-workers who, I came to find out, had shared in her frustrations the previous night as they had been waiting in the parking lot to see Bob's reaction. All in all, we spent about $400 to undo our mistake. But, when we consider that Sue and Bob might represent $25,000 to us over their lifetimes, that money was well spent—especially because I don't think Sue expected to receive as much as we gave her. After Tom had left her home that evening, explaining what we wanted to do to make up for our mistake, he called me later on and left a message, "Dude, she kissed me." Not a bad day, from having someone who wants to chop your head off in the morning to getting literally kissed later that night—a customer service job well done.

My favorite part of the story, however, is that, about a week later, I received an envelope in the mail. Inside was a check made out to Zane's for $400 from Greg, the employee who had originally dealt with Sue, along with a letter of apology. On the memo line of the check, he had written "fuck-up." In his letter, Greg wrote:

Dear Chris—

On February fourteenth I dealt with a prospective "lifetime customer." In those dealings, I, as a Zane's Cycles employee, assured her that we would carry out a simple request. For whatever reason, this small request was forgotten. I realized at the moment the relationship with the customer (as well as her dozen friends) was shattered. Please consider this letter as a formal apology for any inconveniences or headaches I may have caused you or your management. Enclosed is a check for the estimated amount of rebuilding the customer relationship.

Of course, I never cashed that check; in fact, it's in a frame above my desk. The point is that Greg, who still works for me more than ten years later, gets what we're doing at Zane's. Although it cost the business a few hundred dollars, it was worth every dollar to be witness to the top-notch character of an employee like Greg.

• scaling up and branching out •

As we continue to expand as a business, we'll be working even harder to find the best people to staff our positions at Zane's stores across the country. To get there, we'll be using the same formula for success that we've been using for the past thirty years—only modified to fit a bigger scale. Just like at Mitchells , Stew Leonard's, and The Container Store, we won't be changing any of our core practices, only re-creating them and carrying them forward. And as we get bigger and bigger, and continue to employ more and more people, we'll also have to work harder at adapting to the breadth and diversity of personalities and cultures that those employees will bring with them into the workplace. Let's talk more about what this involves in the next chapter.

. 9 .

mix it up

ONE OF THE new realities of business is the paramount requirement that everyone in an organization must be compassionate and accepting of other people and cultures. That can mean people that speak another language or it can mean embracing someone from a younger generation, people of different genders or races, or someone who has a different sexual preference. It just doesn't matter. This is particularly true of an organization like Zane's.

Most bike shops, of course, are filled with men who often spend their days talking about the technical aspects of riding or even dabbling in a bit of profanity. Zane's was always different in this regard—we've always had people of different genders, colors, and sexual preferences on the payroll. But once we expanded beyond our single location, I couldn't personally monitor everyone's behavior to each other anymore—let alone make every decision about whom to hire or fire.

When it comes to hiring new employees or reaching out to that new customer who just walked in the door or even interacting with existing co-workers, everyone in the Zane's organization must embrace the idea that even if someone looks or talks different from you, he or she still represents that same $12,500 opportunity as anybody else. The goal of Zane's is to be a destination where everyone feels welcome. Not only is this just the right way to do things, it makes for good business.

This isn't something that is always self-evident, though; it needs to be taught and woven into the culture of your business. And the principle that needs to be taught is that a foundation for exceptional customer service begins by embracing cultures that may differ from those with which you or your employees are familiar. But what does that have to do with providing extraordinary customer service, you ask? Absolutely everything. I believe that everything in a business is connected in some big cosmic circle; every action has some kind of ripple effect. That means that as you reach out to embrace the diversity in your workforce, you should also be doing the same with your customers.

• overcoming cultural barriers •

One of my personal challenges at Zane's is that I have about twenty employees who speak Spanish as their native language. And regardless of what side of the political debate you stand on, the simple truth is that immigrant workers from all over Central and South America have become a critical resource for companies like Zane's. Without stereotyping them too much, I can say that most of the folks that we employ—all legal and documented immigrants, just so you know—are incredibly hardworking and conscientious about the tasks they have been assigned. They are amazing mechanics and technicians. But we still have language and cultural barriers to overcome on a daily basis.

First off, just because someone speaks Spanish, he or she can't be lumped in with everyone else who speaks that language. Nations like Mexico, Ecuador, and Chile all have different cultural norms that also serve to create barriers and accepted behaviors that we need to work hard at overcoming. It therefore remains a constant challenge to translate the importance of "Reinventing the Wheel"—to get these men and women to appreciate the importance of the lifetime relationships with our customers. Although I might get a nod of the head in response to a story I tell about why we can't afford to forget to include a wrench or a set of instructions along with the bike headed to a recipient, overcoming the language and cultural barriers and really getting my employees to connect with my message remains a challenge.

One of the worst experiences a manager can face is when an employee begins to use language and the possibility of something getting lost in translation as an excuse for why he or she failed to do what was asked. "Did they truly not understand or is this some kind of game?" you're forced to ask yourself. Although I do my best to study language tapes on a daily basis in hopes of improving my skill, I have recognized that I need to bring in the big guns as reinforcement. I look forward to this book being translated into multiple languages so that all my employees will have exactly the same information in their heads that I do. This book will serve as common ground that we can build upon as we continue to expand. With something we can share and build on, voilà, our barriers will begin to melt away.

We also have several bilingual employees who have worked for Zane's for many years who not only help translate our conversations but serve as guides to the rules of the shop. These guys, to me, represent the future of Zane's because they help make language barriers irrelevant. Instead, the most important issue for everyone to focus on is the customer. For example, one of our employees was born in Mexico and has worked for me for fifteen years, during which time I would guess he has built something like 55,000 bikes. There isn't much I can teach him about building bikes and he, in turn, can actually be a mentor on the shop floor to each and every new employee who joins him in our warehouse.

At the same time, one of the guys who works inside the retail shop was born in Colombia but is now an American citizen. His language skills are not only useful in communicating with our Spanish-speaking employees, but he has often used them to smooth over an initial interaction with customers who might prefer talking in Spanish. That means that our guys' language skills are not a barrier but an immensely valuable tool to use in welcoming a whole new segment of customers into the shop. As a matter of fact, I'm always asking both of these guys to bring in their friends to come work for us because of how important multilanguage skills have become in our society today. In other words, I trust both of these guys, just like anyone else working in the shop or on the sales floor, to be on the lookout for new candidates to work at Zane's, no matter what background they may have come from. A fit is a fit, no matter what country you may have been born in.

• gender bender •

When I first began attending industry trade shows more than twenty-five years ago, I was struck by the makeup of the crowds: it was all men. Well, almost all men. The only women in attendance that I ever saw were the scantily clad models brought in by some of the bike manufacturers to draw attention to their booths. It was almost like a scene out of a Vegas nightclub where these young ladies, wearing revealing Lycra racing suits, would saunter around with dozens of panting bike guys in their wake. Of course, you could find this same ratio in most bike shops you walked into at that time as well—if you were a woman hoping to ask another woman for an opinion on a repair or buying a new bike, you were out of luck. As a newcomer to the action, it all just felt odd. I couldn't help shake the feeling that all these guys just didn't accurately reflect who our customers were.

At Zane's, on the other hand, we had a different face to greet our customers: Camille. From the very beginning when I bought the shop, I considered myself just a local kid having fun with bikes. So, I hired my friends to help me whenever possible. It turned out that Camille was a friend of a friend and, as a rider herself, she started coming by the shop to help out behind the counter and with repairs. She was a tough cookie who certainly wasn't intimidated by a bunch of guys; she could spin a wrench as well as she could thread her bike down a patch of rocky single track.

Although I didn't realize it at the time, having Camille on board was a huge differentiating factor for us for reasons that went far beyond her mechanical skill or bike knowledge. For one thing, she brought balance into the shop. Instead of having just a bunch of smelly guys sitting around and telling dirty jokes and whatnot, we were all better behaved with Camille on hand. More important, Camille made our shop far less intimidating to our customers— especially those of the female persuasion. It was almost magical when female customers walked in the store, because, within just a minute or two, they would begin walking over to Camille for help. Camille offered our female customers something I and the other men couldn't. There was a much higher comfort level for them to talk one on one about, say, how a particular piece of clothing fit, obviously something a male salesperson would have a harder time dealing with.

Watching these interactions helped me realize how important it was for us to reflect who our customers were with similar people working behind the counter. Because making connections with our customers was such an important part of our success, how could we ever make that all-important first interaction if the environment they were walking into and the people they needed to speak with immediately intimidated them? The fact was that we were beating our competition because we looked different from them. I grabbed hold of this concept and understood that our continued success depended on delivering unique experiences to any and all customers, no matter their race, gender, or sexual preference. We would embrace the attitude that our bike shop was part of the community we operated in and, as such, our employees would reflect the same makeup as the community.

• embracing customers • with alternative lifestyles

Once we made the conscious decision to take a look at our community and work hard to embrace our customers by employing folks they could relate to, we began uncovering new opportunities we had been blind to before. In particular, we found that, like our competitors, we had overlooked the gay and lesbian community in and around New Haven.

But, perhaps because we were just about the only shop in town that employed women, we began noticing greater numbers of same-sex couples shopping in the store.

At that time, in the late 1980s and early 1990s, alternative lifestyles weren't yet in the mainstream like they are today. Thanks to movies, TV shows, and popular personalities like Rosie O'Donnell and Ellen DeGeneres, things are different today. But even if they weren't, back then as well as now, we approach each of our customers in the same way, making everyone as comfortable with their shopping experience as we can. That means that if a same-sex couple holds hands or kisses each other, we need people working the floor that are not only comfortable with those shows of emotion but also recognize those people for their potential as lifetime customers. If I saw a salesperson walking away from or acting poorly in response to these kinds of actions, that salesperson was on his or her way out the door; we just weren't going to tolerate someone who didn't get what we were all about.

When it came to selling to same-sex couples, though, we discovered something interesting. When you sell to a married heterosexual couple, there is typically a single buying decision that goes on. The couple typically jointly agrees to a purchase, which means you really are trying to complete a single sale. With same-sex couples, though, there were actually two purchasing decisions being made. Although both members of a couple would certainly look to their partner for help and advice, each person was actually acting individually when it came to buying something because each would typically have his or her own credit card or checkbook. Whether it was perusing bikes or accessories, a couple would typically be looking to buy two of everything, although perhaps in a different size or color.

For a salesperson, this was kind of like nirvana: you could actually ring up two sales for the price of one if you played your cards right. This meant, of course, that same-sex couples made for fantastic customers, something we soon moved to capitalize on further by advertising in lifestyle magazines and newspapers and with local events and groups targeted at the same-sex community. For example, we started running ads in the New Haven Gay and Lesbian Newsletter early on. We also became a sponsor for the Gay Men's Chorus. For something like $150 a month, which was far cheaper than running an ad in the Yellow Pages— something that could cost $2,000—we were able to send a targeted message to a very specific segment of the community.

For any business owner who has experienced the frustration of trying to maximize a marketing budget like I have, finding this outlet was like stumbling upon the Holy Grail of advertising. The best part of doing this was not just that we tapped into a whole new customer base, but I would get stopped by both customers and strangers on the street who thanked me for supporting their organizations. The gay and lesbian community is hugely networked and word quickly spread about the kind of business we ran, which just opened up more and more doors for us.

We did, however, go through what, in time, proved to be an ironic experience with a gay employee we hired early on named Mark. Although we were as supportive of Mark as we could be, he was somewhat troubled and quite simply wasn't performing well or reflecting the values that we continue to demand from all of Zane's employees. As a result, I fired him.

You might imagine my surprise, when a few weeks after I let him go, my lawyer received a summons: Mark was suing us for discrimination. He claimed that we fired him because he was gay. At the hearing in front of a judge, Mark's attorney led off by flatly stating that we fired Mark after we learned that he was gay.

"Not true," I said in response. "We all knew Mark was gay from the day we hired him."

"How did you know?" the judge asked me.

"For one, he was quite open about it," I said. "For example, he had a big rainbow sticker on the bumper of his car."

Turning to Mark, the judge asked, "Is this true?" Mark just nodded.

The judge quickly dismissed the suit and even took a few minutes to dress down Mark for unfairly trying to play the sexual identity card against us. As punishment, Mark ended up having to pay all of our legal bills as well as his own.

Looking back at our embrace of the same-sex community, there is a particular metaphor I like to use when it comes to making effective inroads with new customers: it all begins with a snowflake. Then, as it picks up traction, it grows into a snowball. Finally, with the momentum in full swing, that snowball becomes an avalanche. This is exactly what happened to us: all of a sudden, not only did our sales to same-sex couples begin to skyrocket, we saw a surge in interest from the community in working for us.

Today, I would estimate that out of every twenty-five bikes we sell, at least three of those bikes are bought by same-sex couples. In other words, this isn't just an insignificant sliver for us—this is big business. And it is amazing that even though we have been advertising and supporting this community for more than twenty years, we continue to be the only bike shop that does so. Although I'm happy to keep an eye on any good ideas my competition might come up with, I'm just as glad that they have failed to capitalize on the opportunities brought about by embracing the alternative lifestyle community.

• embracing new opportunities •

As we have worked hard at making ourselves accessible to each and every demographic slice you can think of, we've also found that our investments in earlier years have begun paying off in new ways that have really brought home the concept of lifetime customers. What I mean by this is that one of the faster growing customer segments we have is made up of older riders. What makes this interesting is not that we have begun some new outreach into the senior and retired communities, but that these are the folks who, twenty years ago, were buying bikes for their kids.

Now that their kids have moved on to college and beyond, these fifty-and-sixty-something-year-old customers are returning to us to find ways to explore their freedom just like their kids had before them. When these folks come into the store, they tell us, "I remember having such a great experience buying from you before, so I thought, what the heck, that's where I'm going to buy a bike for myself." At the same time, we have continued our relationship with the Southern Connecticut Cycling Club, which sponsors group tours that cater to more recreational riders—which, in turn, require exactly the kinds of bikes that we sell. Working with folks like this, we can help our customers choose bikes that are suitable for flatter trails and roads rather than bikes that might be more appropriate for mountain biking or racing. Again, for us, it's always about finding the ways to make those initial and critical connections to our customers so that we can deliver them a shopping experience they won't find anyplace else.

> We gain a lot of credibility with older customers when they see us at an auction for Breast Cancer Awareness, for example, because they recognize that our goal is to become a pillar of the community. My competitors, on the other hand, most of whom are still stocked with young tattooed and pierced guys, remain intimidating for most of this older crowd.

We've also attracted a great deal of attention and awareness of our brand within the older age bracket because of our community outreach and nonprofit efforts. We gain a lot of credibility with older customers when they see us at an auction for Breast Cancer Awareness, for example, because they recognize that our goal is to become a pillar of the community. My competitors, on the other hand, most of whom are still stocked with young tattooed and pierced guys, remain intimidating for most of this older crowd. Why would they expect to be treated well and listened to at the hippie bike messenger hangout? That's not to say we don't have our own share of tattooed and pieced employees, but we also have folks like myself who are there to bridge the gap and serve as someone with whom these customers might be more comfortable interacting.

• finding our national niche •

As we continue our plans to extend the Zane's brand across the country, we will continue to be on the lookout for new niches into which we can expand—always mindful of finding ways to reflect the faces and character of the community we move into. It will be crucial for every Zane's employee to recognize that our continued success as a business is largely a result of our open-mindedness and ability to capitalize on selling to demographic slices that others may have overlooked. I need my managers to embrace the new opportunities their customers bring to them in our new markets and to tap their own personal networks to keep our talent pipeline full of great and diverse people.

Everything we have done in Branford serves as our playbook about the kinds of things we know work well, such as embracing diversity of race and culture, that we need to apply to the operations of any store flying the Zane's flag. We need to amplify each and every message that applies to our original store so that it applies to 100 stores or more. Let's talk more about how we plan to do that in the next chapter.

· 10 ·

think nationally, act locally

ONE OF THE major challenges lying ahead at Zane's as we go national is that, similar to big-time competitors like Walmart or even companies we'd love to emulate such as The Container Store, everyone in the organization will need to work even harder to protect the culture and keep our focus as we evolve from a small company into a large one. In other words, we need to overcome the challenge of scaling up from a single location into multiple stores spread across the country without sacrificing what has carried us this far. As we get bigger and bigger, we could easily convince ourselves that we need to start doing things differently. While you might be able to go into every Walmart or Starbucks in the country and have it look and feel the same way, not every business that goes national has been able to perfect that kind of scaling challenge.

The principles of building relationships and selling experiences apply to more than just small businesses; they can work no matter how big our business becomes. And that means that each and every Zane's employee needs to embrace each of the lessons we have discussed in the first nine chapters of this book.

Chapter One: Maintain a constant focus on the business we're in. Stay passionate about the experience and don't become overwhelmed by the products we sell. It's not the business of bikes but the business of fun.

Chapter Two: Focus on building lifetime relationships—with each customer who walks in, regardless of whether that store is in Branford, Connecticut, or in Timbuktu. Work to ensure we continue to collect on the $12,500 by constantly reminding ourselves about the lifetime value rather than the transaction at hand.

Chapter Three: Strengthen the legs of the stool by developing additional offerings that allow the bowl of quarters to appear even larger. By providing more service than seems reasonable, knowing that customers self-regulate, Zane's can continue to break away from the pack, creating lifetime customers.

Chapter Four: Supporting programs and building a brand in the minds of future customers guarantees we'll be the top-of-mind choice when it's time for them to make an investment. Constantly looking forward and building a solid foundation for the brand will insulate us against competitors long before the customers surface.

Chapter Five: Keep looking for a new niche. Explore opportunities to build new relationships in a nontraditional business by keeping open to new and different ways of servicing the market, all while building in unique service offerings.

Chapter Six: By changing up the game, we're keeping the competition off balance. If our competitors are focused on our next move, then they aren't creating programs to strengthen their brand. Understanding that it's our game and we can subsequently changes the rules, we have the opportunity to control the moves required to build lifetime customers.

Chapter Seven: By fixing what isn't broken, we can build our company on our terms rather than reacting to a crisis. Continuous improvement ensures we are never on autopilot, allowing us to see and re-engineer offerings to best fit the customers' needs.

Chapter Eight: Hiring nice people and training them about our stuff will allow the culture to survive. Creating long-term problems by finding short-term solutions by hiring the wrong person for the job is a liability we can't afford. The process of building a team that enjoys each other's company will create an environment that the customer will appreciate and recognize as unique.

Chapter Nine: By not just looking at what we are but understanding that we live and work in a multicultural society, we can embrace the differences and learn the needs of each community. Building a service offering specific to individual needs will allow us to connect and build relationships that will secure our success throughout a multicultural community.

• strength in numbers •

Not a day goes by when I don't think back to the expensive and humbling lessons I learned from opening the Zane's Outdoor shop, our first foray into expanding our business. Today, more than twenty-five years later, I've finally grown my skin thick enough to the point where I can look back and admit my missteps and mistakes. And with Zane's Cycles about to embark on a nationwide expansion, I wouldn't trade my experiences with Zane's Outdoor for anything. I look at those ten weeks as the most successful $100,000 failure ever.

Why? Because I can use that experience to steer me toward making the best decisions as we expand our organization today and in the future, as well as remind myself of all the lessons I learned in what *not* to do—namely, forgetting what business we're really in.

No doubt, one of the biggest mistakes I made with Zane's Outdoor was thinking arrogantly enough to believe that I could do it all on my own. In my defense, I was young and ambitious and I thought the more I collaborated and sought advice from others, the slower things would go. In learning the errors of my ways, I've come to recognize the strength that comes from working on a team with individuals who are not only talented in their own right but also bring a variety of skills to the table. Tom, for example, now understands more about running the day-to-day retail operation than I ever will. That's why he's now in charge of much of the planning associated with expanding our retail operations. Along those same lines, I am using the rules I talked about back in chapter eight to fill the entire organization from top to bottom with not only friendly people but also those who have the capability to work independently and who bring expertise in everything from identifying the best real estate opportunities to running the information technology operations of a national business. As I've come to realize, if I try to micromanage every aspect of our expansion, we'll be looking at a failure of catastrophic proportions. But, if I can keep my eye on the big picture and guide my team toward the end zone, we'll have our hands on the handlebars of the finest bike retailing operation in the United States.

We also have great examples like The Container Store's extensive employee training and Harrah's intimate understanding of lifetime customer value, to learn and maybe even steal a few new ideas from. These companies, which are already national, continue to drink from the same bowl of customer-focused Kool-Aid that I do. Basically, we've all bought into the same vision and we're moving forward together, convinced we're not headed for a cliff. Using feedback from our fellow devotees of customer-centric strategies such as these, we'll be able to cut down on the mistakes we might have made otherwise and, at the same time, minimize the amount of risk we face when we go after new opportunities.

For example, we would never have had the insight to roll out a (Customer Relationship Management) system based on the four customer categories devised by Martin Mende that I talked about back in chapter one without a great network in place. In other words, we now have the intellectual capital to go with our ambition to become something the world of business has never seen before: a true customer-focused organization built from the ground up.

The notion that Zane's as an organization is embarking on a mission to take personalized, one-on-one customer service to a different scale has excited more than just my employees: it has also juiced up the best minds on the planet when it comes to thinking about customer service theory. Academic researchers from the Center for Services Leadership at Arizona State University, consultants from the Peppers & Rogers Group, and my friend Len Berry at Texas A&M University are all chomping at the bit to see how some of their textbook theories get implemented. I consider all of these folks my friends and advisors and they have somewhat of a vested interest in seeing Zane's grow and expand because the only companies they have to study at this point are companies that are already national.

For instance, Gary Loveman, the former Harvard Business School professor who now heads up Harrah's Entertainment (which operates the Harrah's and Caesars casinos in Las Vegas, along with forty-six other casinos around the country), started implementing his customer service theories in an organization that, with 120,000 employees, was already enormous. But the researchers have been watching us for fifteen years, as we grew from $2 million in revenue and became a champion for the idea of selling customer experiences instead of bikes. Now, we're about to climb up on a bigger and even more ambitious stage.

Zane's will be one of a kind because we are a blank slate of sorts—putting into practice many of the theories people like Len have been writing about for years. But, instead of spending our time thinking about how to overcome hurdles in putting these practices into place like Gary has had to do, we'll be spending our time blasting ahead and finding the best and most efficient ways to implement processes from the very beginning that focus on our customers. That's why they are all just about as excited as I am to see how we put the pieces together.

In the end, one of my personal goals is to show that every company, particularly large national ones, needs to start thinking of customer service as a profit creator, not just a cost sink. Let's face it, my competitors are headed toward an iceberg that they don't even yet realize exists, and they may not even be in a position to react and change their course for another ten years. Knowing that we, too, have plenty of challenges to solve in the coming years, given the team we have assembled and the lessons we've learned, we're hopeful we're prepared for the long ride.

index

a

academic theories, 155–157, 198–199
advertising. *See* marketing
Alpha Dogs (Fenn), 94
American Demographics, 63
Arizona State University Center for
    Service Leadership, 155, 198–199
attention span, 22

b

Berry, Len, 155, 198–199
Big Wheel Sale, 128–129, xvi
brand development, 26–28, 55–56,
    63–64, 80, 82–85, 109, 190–191,
    195
business
    culture, 193
    differentiation of, 6–7, 150–151
    expansion of, 92–93, 111–113, 118,
        133–135, 176–177, 191–194
    growth, 92–93, 100, 111–113
    opportunity recognition, 94–96,
        100, 191–192, 195
    principles, 116
    type of, 7–11
buying decisions, 35–37, 63, 186–187

c

capital investments, 105–106
categorizing customers, 12–13, 15–22,
    198
charities, 86–88
commitment, demonstration of,
    46–49, 113

communication, 19–20, 113, 137–142,
    145–151, 155–157, 172
community ties, 189–191
    building, 80–85
    investing in, 86–90
competition
    advantages of, 130–133
    customers, luring from, 72–75
    customer service and, 116–119
    eliminating, 59–61, 65, 129, 132
    employees, luring from, 122–125
    expansion and, 133–135
    game of, 115, 119–122, 130–133, 195
    goal of, 133
    pressure on, 126–129
    pricing and, 6, 118
competitive insulation, 132
connections, business, 103–105
connection with customers, 11–17, 29,
    33–34, 149, 150, 153–154
continuous improvement, 137–142,
    145–151, 155–157, 195, 198
corporate rewards programs. *See* spe-
    cial markets
customer database, 141–144
customer relationships
    building, 23, 26–29, 40–44, 50–52,
        58, 85, 90–92
    cementing, 90, 145
    nature of, 78
    personalizing, 44–45
    salvaging, 1–5, 40–43, 171–176
customers
    attention span, 22

attention to, 108
business decisions, driving, 155
categories of, 12–13, 15–22, 198
communication with, 19–20, 113,
137–142, 145–151, 155–157, 172
competition, keeping from, 72–75
decision making and, 35–37, 63,
186–187
diversity of, 185–189
educating, 76
employee relationship with, 141
evaluating, 151–152
feedback from, 137–142, 145–151,
155–157, 171–172, 198
investment in, 38–39
lifetime value of, 32–34, 46–47,
189–191, 194
loss of, 40–41
loyalty of, 40
marketing and (*See* marketing)
older, 189–191
patience with, 21–22
preferences of, 13
retention of, 40–44, 46–49, 62–63,
151–154
self-regulation of, 39, 194
theft and, 163–166
trust and, 32, 37, 46–49, 58, 163
customer satisfaction, 36–37, 42–43,
100, 112, 113. *See also* customer
relationships
customer service
buying decisions and, 35–37, 63,
186–187
as competitive edge, 116–119
diversity and, 180, 185–189
feedback and, 137–142, 145–151,
155–157, 171–172, 198
quality of, 9–11, 31, 63, 134–135,
154, 194
study of, 133–134, 155, 198–199
vs. low prices, 5–7
customer *vs.* partner, 67–68

d

database, customer, 141–144
demographics, 189–191. *See also*
diversity
differentiation, of business, 6–7, 150–151
diversity

of customers, 185–189
customer service and, 180
of employees, 179–183, 187–189
gender and, 183–185
language and cultural barriers,
181–183
older customers and, 189
success and, 191–192, 196

e

Edmundson, Brad, *American Demographics,* 63
emotional connection, 16, 33–34, 149,
150, 153–154
employees, 106
accountability of, 170–172
competition, luring from, 122–125
diversity of, 179–183, 187–189
empowering, 169–172, 197
expansion and, 176–177
finding, 166–169
flexibility of, 162–165
gender of, 183–185
hiring criteria and, 160–162
mistakes, learning from, 173–176
quality of, 159–160, 196
relationship with customers, 141
theft from, 166
training, 153
expansion, 92, 93, 111–113, 118, 133–
135, 176–177, 191–194
experiences, selling, 7–11, 62, 115,
116, 199

f

failure, learning from, 173–176,
196–197
feedback, 113, 137–142, 145–151,
155–157, 171–172, 198
Fenn, Donna
Alpha Dogs, 94
"Leader of the Pack," 56, 111
flat tire insurance program, 72–78,
119–120

g

gift certificates, 31
giveaways, 37–38, 85, 120–121
"Golden Carrot," 112
goodwill, 37–38, 81

guarantees and warranties, 56–61, 64–65, 67, 69–72, 117

h

Harrah's, 42, 198–199
hiring criteria, 160–162
home-delivery, 77–78
Hopkins, Tom, 20–21
Hug Your Customers (Mitchell), 9–11
Hug Your People (Mitchell), 9

i

improvement, continuous, 137–142, 145–151, 155–157, 195, 198
inclusivity. *See* diversity
insulation, competitive, 132
inventory, distribution of, 111–113
investment, customer service as, 134–135

j

judgments about customers, 12–13, 15–22, 198

k

Karbo, Joe, *A Lazy Man's Ways to Riches,* 46, 70
Kling, George, 103–105

l

A Lazy Man's Ways to Riches (Karbo), 46, 70
"Leader of the Pack" (Fenn), 56, 111
lifetime relationships
    from best value package, 61–68
    building, 50–52, 85, 90–92, 194
    marketing and, 53
lifetime service guarantees, 56–61
lifetime trade-in program, 50–53, 90
lifetime value of customers, 32–34, 46–47, 189–191, 194
listening to customers, 113, 137–142, 145–151, 155–157, 172
logos, 26–28. *See also* brand development
Loveman, Gary, 42–43, 199

m

Mancini, Dino, 25–26
marketing, 44–45, 63–64, 66

creativity in, 121–122
customers and, 12–14, 187
differentiation from, 55–56
goodwill and, 81
lifetime relationships and, 53
technology and, 121–122, 135
mass marketing, 12–13
Mende, Martin, 12–14, 155, 198
Mitchell, David, 40
Mitchell, Jack, 43
    Hug Your Customers, 9–11
    Hug Your People, 9
Mitchells, 9, 176
multicultural society. *See* diversity

n

neighborhood ties, 189–191
    building, 80–85
    investing in, 86–90
networking, 103–105
not-for-profit organizations, 86–88

o

opportunity recognition, 94–96, 100, 191–192, 195

p

partner *vs.* customer, 67–68
patience, with customers, 21–22, 107–108
Peppers & Rogers Group, 198
"pointing north," 162–166, 169
premiums. *See* special markets
price protection guarantee, 69–72
pricing, 5–7, 63

r

relationships
    building, 23, 26–29, 40–44, 50–52, 58, 85, 90–92
    cementing, 90, 145
    maintaining, 68
    nature of, 78
    personalizing, 44–45
    salvaging, 1–5, 40–43, 171–176
    with vendors, 65–68
reputation, 61
respect, 18
rewards programs. *See* special markets

s

sales staff. *See* employees
satisfaction, customer, 36–37, 42–43,
    100, 112, 113. *See also* customer
    relationships
scaling challenge, 193–194
selling experiences, 7–11, 62, 115,
    116, 199
service, customer
    buying decisions and, 35–37, 63,
        186–187
    as competitive edge, 116–119
    diversity and, 180, 185–189
    feedback and, 137–142, 145–151,
        155–157, 171–172, 198
    quality of, 9–11, 31, 63, 134–135,
        154, 194
    study of, 133–134, 155, 198–199
    vs. low prices, 5–7
service guarantees and warranties,
    56–61, 64–65, 67, 69–72, 117
special markets, 95–102
    breaking into, 102–110
    expansion in, 111–113
    trade shows and, 102–103
Stew Leonard's, 134, 176
store layout, 14–15, 27–30, 73–74,
    91–92
suppliers, 65–68
surveys, 137, 145–146, 151–152

t

technology
    customer relationships and, 142, 145

marketing and, 121–122, 135
Texas A&M University, 133–134, 198–199
The Container Store, 134, 176, 193,
    198
theft, 163–166
theories, academic, 155–157, 198–199
trade-in program, 50–53, 90
trust, building, 37, 46–49, 58, 163

u

Underhill, Paco, *Why We Buy: The Science of Buying*, 73–74

v

value of customers, lifetime, 32–34
value propositions, 66
    evaluating, 77–78
    flat tire insurance program, 72–78,
        119–120
    lifetime service guarantee, 56–61
    price protection guarantee, 69–72
vendors, 65–68

w

walking the walk, 46–49
warranties and guarantees, 56–61,
    64–65, 67, 69–72, 117
Why We Buy: The Science of Buying
    (Underhill), 73–74
workforce. *See* employees

z

The Zane Foundation, 86–90
Zane's Outdoor, 93, 196, xiii–xvii

about the author

AT AGE 46, Christopher J. Zane is already a thirty-year veteran of the retail bicycle industry. His story includes getting a state tax ID number at age 12, buying his first bike shop at age 16, and building Zane's Cycles into the largest bicycle shop in Connecticut by the age of 30. Today, Zane's Cycles is one of the largest retail bicycle stores in the nation.

Zane's unique approach to marketing includes strategies such as continual learning, the lifetime value of a customer, guerrilla marketing, bootstrapping, community relations, cost-controlled customer service, and image branding. He has positioned himself at the forefront of the industry by continuously setting standards in customer loyalty and creative marketing.

Since 1985, Zane has been accumulating awards and accolades such as the BBB Award of Recognition for Customer Service/Outstanding Business Practices; one of "the 30 most influential people in the bicycle industry"; North America's Best Bicycle Retailer, *North American Bicyclist Magazine*; Mass Mutual Blue Chip Enterprise Initiative Award; 2006 Customer First Award, *Fast Company Magazine* and the

2006 Connecticut "Retailer of the Year." Zane's Cycles currently holds the status of Trek Bicycle Co.'s largest dealer worldwide. Most recently, Chris was inducted into the Junior Achievement Business Leader Hall of Fame, named the 2008 Customer Champion, *1to1 magazine*, and the 2009 CT Climate Change Leadership Award.

Zane's cutting-edge marketing techniques have been used as case studies in more than a dozen college textbooks worldwide and has been the subject of several articles in publications such as The *Harvard Business Review, Inc.* magazine, *the Associated Press, Fortune* magazine, *The New York Times* and *The Wall Street Journal,* as well as being profiled in *Alpha Dogs*, a HarperCollins bestseller by Donna Fenn. Zane has served as Quinnipiac University's Entrepreneur in Residence and he is frequently featured on WCBS's, *"The Wall Street Journal's* Small Business Report" with Joe Connolly.

A sought-after speaker, Zane has presented to individual companies and at numerous conferences: Yale University's Business and Economic Forum; Quis 9 International Marketing Symposium; The Conference Board; Inc's Annual Growing the Company Conference; Inc's Annual CEO Symposium; WCBS Newsradio 88 Business Breakfast Forum, and ASU's Compete Through Services Symposium, where he was the highest rated speaker. He is currently a board member of several organizations, including The Sachem Bank (IO) and ASU's The Center for Services Leadership.